THE GOSPEL ACCORDING TO JOSH

A 28-YEAR GENTILE BAR MITZVAH

JOSH RIVEDAL

Skookum Hill Publishing
ASTORIA, NEW YORK

Skookum Hill Publishing
2601 29th Street, Suite 3
Astoria, NY 11102

Thematic Editors: Jeanette Shaw & Suzanne Paire
Copyeditor: Pamela Guerrieri
Cover Design: Jose Putman
Book Layout: Joel Friedlander, Tracy R. Atkins, & Josh Rivedal

This book describes the real experiences of real people. The author has disguised the identities of some but none of these changes has affected the truthfulness and accuracy of his story.

Ordering Information:
Quantity sales. Special discounts are available on quantity purchases by corporations, associations, and others. For details, contact the "Special Sales Department" at the address above. Contact the author directly at http://gospeljosh.com for special fund-raising opportunities for charitable organizations.

The Gospel According to Josh/ Josh Rivedal -- 1st ed.
ISBN 978-0-9860338-0-3

Acknowledgements

David Nathan Scott, Suzanne Paire, Holly Rivedal, Jacob Rivedal, Erica Chiarelli, Joe Chiarelli, Josh Gaboian, Brent Buell, David Sitt, Mary Harris, Ada Gonzalez, Brian Kornet, Matt Hoverman, the Kozlowski family, the Cocco family, the Lichtmann family, the Pehrson family, Jenny Rietveld, Michael Roderick, Lorenzo Lebrija, PJ Walsh, Mary Dimino, Deric Rosenblatt, Chad Gaudet, Ralph Landi, Chris Delmond, Craig Carnelia, Meridoc Burkhardt, Colleen deVeer, Hogan Gorman, Katie Klaus, Jeff Tanski, Chiara Montalto, Roberto Ragone, Todd Wharton, Mike Bauer, Namakula Mu, Jami Saracino, Jesse Cline, Patrick Ward, Michael Wolk, Chip Roberts, Colleen Healy, Amanda Healy, Efrem Epstein, Camilla Ross, Paulette Rao,

and

Douglas Rivedal

Though you may hear me holler
And you may see me cry
I'll be dogged, sweet baby
If you gonna see me die.

Life is fine! Fine as wine! Life is fine!

–Langston Hughes, *Life is Fine*

ONE

....

AN EPILOGUE PART ONE— SORT OF

There I was at William Woods University in the middle of Missouri, decked out in a long-sleeved, blue flannel shirt and faded boot-cut jeans, standing behind a podium under a warm spotlight in front of a few hundred wide-eyed college students and some anxious faculty members, vocally paralyzed and desperately wishing I could gather myself just long enough to string together a few coherent sentences for this room full of academics.

I felt like I was living that awful nightmare—you know, the one where you're standing in front of a large group of people ready to say something epic and groundbreaking, except somehow you left your house not only forgetting to wear pants but your underpants as well, prompting the crowd to point, laugh, and throw rotten tomatoes at you with their free, non-pointing hand.

However, this moment of paralysis I was having on stage at William Woods University was all too real. I was definitely wearing pants, and this being November, tomatoes were out of season.

I had never gone stiff in front of a crowd in my entire life. By the tender age of six, I was already wooing handkerchief-waving old ladies and a church congregation of more than five hundred as a song and not-so-much dance man. Performing on stage was as second nature to me as breathing, eating, and sleeping.

But standing next to that podium and sweating under those lights, I began to experience what seemed like some kind of spiritual, out-of-body experience... which would have been awesome if I were drinking peyote tea in New Mexico with Tommy Chong and a psychoactive Sonoran Desert toad. But God knows I'm not that lucky, and whatever transcendent experience I was having was happening at the worst possible time.

I could almost see a part of me floating above my head, finding its way to a seat in the front row— eagerly anticipating whatever was going to happen next. It was like that scene from *The Adventures of Tom Sawyer* when Tom and Huck were sitting in the rafters watching their own funeral. Except this wasn't supposed to be my funeral. This was my resurrection party, and I desperately wanted to celebrate with the auditorium full of spectators in front of me.

But with every silent second that passed, my credibility and grip on mystique and intrigue loosened, especially with the younger students whose hands were reaching for the smartphones on their hips to fill the time being sucked away by the lifeless question mark of a man standing before them.

And it was here that the much-needed role of cheerleader was filled by the usually ornery and disapproving voices in my head. If my brain was put up to a sonar machine, these voices would sound much like a cacophony of a Bible-quoting ball of religiosity due to my evangelical formative years, a wannabe ghetto-fabulous street thug due to my affinity for early 1990s hip-hop, and a Spanglish *mala palabra*-spewing joker as a result of working in restaurants with Mexican and Ecuadorian line cooks.

(*—Speak! Make a joyful noise unto the Lord...—*)
(*—You got this, my dude, for shizzle...—*)

(—*¡Sí se puede, güey!*—)

Following this short bit of internal dialogue, my joints began to thaw and dexterity returned to my hands. I dabbed at my eyes with the knuckle of each forefinger, licked my lips, and couldn't help but reflect on everything that had happened to me in the last two years. I was lucky to be alive and standing on that stage. This trippy and reminiscent stupor was quite possibly the longest fifteen seconds of my life.

Just as I regained my ability to speak, I went into the front left pocket of my jeans and removed my wallet. Inside was a tattered piece of computer paper folded over four times, which I quickly unfurled and read to myself. Scribbled on that piece of paper were three things that kept me alive only ten months earlier. I crouched over, just slightly, to drop the paper into my book bag sitting at my feet behind the podium.

"How's everybody doing?" I asked my audience while wiping small gobs of sweat mixed with hair wax from my temples. "So basically, you know, I've performed the one-man show you just saw, *The Gospel According to Josh*, outside of the college arena quite a bit. It all started as a piece of theatre in New York City, where people, like, really dug the comedy of it. But truthfully much of the initial response I heard was in whispers. People were talking about the end, about my father's suicide, and what they thought they knew about him—and what they thought they knew about suicide. But I knew what they were saying wasn't true. It was incorrect.

"What I was hearing—and bear with me on this—reminded me of how we as children first learned about sex. Which was how? On the playground, right? Sadly, my playground was particularly slow, bless our little hearts, and till the age of twelve, I thought..."

(—*Even a fool who keeps silent is considered wise...*—)
(—*Do not tell them that story, dawg...*—)
(—*They're going to think you're, como se llama? Estúpido...*—)

"... a Fallopian tube was something people brought to a water park so they didn't drown."

(—*You see... they laughed.*—)
(—*At you. Not with you, homeboy.*—)

"But fortunately with sex, we catch up and learn what we need to know in school. So by the age of fifteen, sixteen, we learn what we need to know, though some of you delinquents in the back still have no idea what's going on. I'm just kidding; you guys are alright back there."

GET ON WITH THE STORY, BROTHA!

Right about now you might be wondering, "Why, Josh? Why are you telling me all this? What could you possibly gain by revealing yourself to the world, by choosing to tell this story?" And to that I say, "What story? I never promised to tell you a story." But I'll make a deal with you. If you finish all your dinner and wash your face, I will tell you a tale of struggle and survival, a gospel account of a young man's passage into manhood—his twenty-eight-year Gentile bar mitzvah, a view into the life of a chronically unhappy artist and religious expat who wanted nothing more than to find the meaning in his father's suicide and his own "happily ever after"... only to go through three circles of hell and a near-death experience to get everything he had always wanted. Now put your arms and legs inside the vehicle. You're in for a bumpy ride.

TWO

··

A PROLOGUE PART ONE—
THE GREAT WHITE HOPE

Nineteen eighty-four was a monumental year in the annals of history. In the National Basketball Association, Michael Jordan got drafted by the Chicago Bulls. The U.S. Space Shuttle Discovery took its maiden voyage. George Orwell's novel finally came to fruition. And Joshua Stuart Rivedal was born in Trenton, New Jersey, to proud-ish parents Douglas and Holly.

Douglas, an overweight and socially awkward man (picture a cross between Al Bundy from *Married...with Children* and Andy Sipowicz from *NYPD Blue*), worked for the state of New Jersey as a low-level employee in the Department of Environmental Protection. He was underworked and underpaid.

My mother, Holly, a shy and sheltered woman (physically imagine a Lynda Carter type) originally from a small town in northwestern Pennsylvania, was a meek Christian schoolteacher turned homemaker.

Much of what I remember about her from those early days included the lopsided haircuts she gave me, the neon pink and blue-checkered shorts she sewed for me, and bedtime readings of all *The Chronicles of Narnia* books. And the fights with Douglas. Peppered into their usual discourse were words like "pig," "fat," and "stupid," and no car ride or dinner was complete without one of them telling the other to shut up. I knew from an early age that they were unhappy. They never spent time together and never said simple words like "I love you," to each other, like the parents of my friends from church.

Erica, my sister and Irish twin, arrived exactly 381 days ahead of me. For the first few years of my life, she served as my third parent. She would try to clothe and feed me, much to my dismay. And whenever there were eggs cooking or whenever my diaper was filled to capacity, Erica would scold me in her broken English that, "Jow-a poopies." Embarrassed and ashamed, I retired my diaper for good at the age of fourteen months and moved on to the big boy-potty, which I've been using ever since. I still can't bring myself to eat egg products.

And then there's my brother Jacob, who magically came home from the hospital with my mother when I was four and a half. I was skeptical about his legitimacy as a true sibling, mainly because he was pretty fat, he smelled kinda funny, and I had never seen him before. But he *did* resemble everyone else in the family. After a few weeks of living with us, it didn't look like he was going to leave. So, I had no choice but to accept him as one from the tribe called Rivedal. And like my sister before me, I appointed myself as a third parent to Jacob, teaching him how to tie his shoes and how to properly open a Capri Sun without the straw puncturing the back of the pouch, juice spilling all over the place—the important stuff.

We were sweet, well-behaved, bigheaded little children. When the three of us were ages six, five, and six months Emmanuel, the deaf guy at our church (every church has one, so that bored children can watch the Sunday morning sermon in flamboyant and awkward sign language) asked my mother, "Did it hurt?"

"Did what hurt?" my mother asked, perplexed at such a vague question.

"Your children—they have such large, round heads," he answered without skipping a beat.

Lucky for us, our heads stayed the same size while we grew into our adult bodies.

Operation Freedom

Do you ever wonder whether your parents really wanted children, or if you were some sort of obligation either because of religious guilt, a persuasive spouse, or a rudimentary knowledge of the Roe v. Wade laws? I'm not sure that my father ever wanted children—make that I'm not sure he ever really wanted *me*.

Even before I could walk, my father found ways to crush my spirit and batter my little body over "misdemeanors" like spilling milk, talking back, or having to go to the bathroom during church. Family legend has it that when I was a few months old, my mother left me at home with my father while she went out to run some errands. A few hours later she came back to find me in my crib huffing and puffing under a pile of six winter coats. As an adult I asked him why on earth he would do something like this. "You should've seen the look on your face. It was the only way I could get you to stop crying," he said, wearing his highly questionable parenting skills as a badge of honor.

When I was six, my folks took me to play on the monkey bars for the first time. My father, who was helping me across, thought I needed some tough love so he let go of me halfway through. I swung down so hard that I dislocated my shoulder and fell to the ground screaming in pain. "What are you crying about?" he asked, incredulous that I had the sheer audacity to hurt myself. "I'm not taking you to the hospital. *L.A. Law* is on in ten minutes. I am not going to miss my Jimmy Smits for you." He manually popped my shoulder back into place right there on the playground. A small part of me doesn't blame him. That Jimmy Smits was a bit of a hunk— the platonic Latino-man-crush of a good portion of the male species living in the 1980s.

My breaking point with my father came when I was eleven years old. We were building our own house in the suburbs of New Jersey to get away from our one-bedroom palace in Trenton. I always helped my father—to prove my worth to him and myself. My jobs included helping install the fiberglass insulation, putting up sheetrock, and cutting down trees with a hacksaw and ax, turning them into firewood for the wood stove that would heat our new home exclusively year-round. On this particular day, I volunteered to water the brown grass that grew in small patches in our yard. I admit, I was a little careless about the job at hand (probably because I was eleven and easily distracted by flittering butterflies and an assortment of tall sassafras and oak trees with thick branches I could climb) and I accidentally flooded the neighbor's lawn.

Noticing the new Josh-made lake next door, my father went berserk. He pulled me inside by my ear and whipped my back ten times with one-inch thick copper electrical wire. The skin on my back was open. I had welts and was bleeding profusely.

Following this physical and verbal beating from my father, I retreated to my bedroom angry and disappointed in myself for not finding the courage to fight back. Leaning against my bunk bed, what little ego I had left now deflated, I wrapped a belt around my neck and squeezed so hard that the blood vessels popped underneath the skin and left a red ringlet around my neck that forced me to wear turtlenecks for a week. And it was then that I realized getting out of that house and away from that tyrant was now a matter of life and death. It was time for my little self to come up with a plan to make my escape.

"I've got it," I said, practically screaming while in this self-imposed exile in my bedroom still nursing the lacerations on my back. "I'm going to get by through middle school and high school on my awkward charm and burgeoning good looks. After that, I'll get a job, get a car, escape this stupid town and go straight to Hollywood... I'm going to call it 'Operation Freedom.' Phase One: Middle School, Step One: Join the School Choir."

My plan had everything—triumph, redemption, and revenge. Stephen J. Cannell could not have crafted a finer script.

The Messianic Promise of a Magic Box

As a family, we belonged to a born-again, evangelical Baptist church whose uncompromising ideologies I've tried to distance myself from for as long as I can remember.

It wasn't just that we went there five times a week or that I went to school there from kindergarten to eighth grade. It wasn't just that we weren't allowed to participate in such enjoyable activities as dancing, drinking alcohol, swearing, impure thoughts, and secular non-Christian music. No. Verily I say unto thee the thing that chapped my hide, the thing that really killed me was the fact that this church preached fire and brimstone against the evils of television and Hollywood, because as far back as I can remember, I yearned to taste the sweet nectar of movie stardom.

As a four-year-old, I filled my afternoons living vicariously through the first positive male role models in my life—B.A. Baracus and the rest of the A-Team, Fred Gwynne, also known as Herman Muenster, Lee Majors from *Fall Guy*, Jan Michael Vincent from *Airwolf*, and Fred Sanford from *Sanford and Son*. These guys were the titans of television. Each lived in a fantastical world of adventure, drama, and comedy; and I wanted to be just like them. In television, I found an escape—a magical box that guaranteed that no matter how dire someone's circumstances, everything would work out nice and neat in sixty minutes or less. Everyone got their "happily ever after," and I wanted mine too. As a five-year-old, having a dream about playing the new love interest of Joanna Kerns on the television show *Growing Pains* was the final clincher. Hollywood would serve as the route for *my* escape from my mean, old father and the crazy, religious world in which I lived. It would be a fairytale ending. My own Promised Land.

THREE

....

A PROLOGUE PART TWO—
THE JOSH STRIKES BACK

With the tenacity of a ninja and the focus of a Jedi, I stayed on course with my escape plan by joining the school *and* church choirs. I also decided I was going to try out for my fifth grade school musical, inspired by the acclaim my father received for his solo career at church. He sang a mean rendition of the Christian country music song, "Take off Those Rags, Lazarus," and the church audiences ate him up. They loved him. During his heyday, he was like the church's weird, overweight version of Justin Bieber.

There was one man in particular who enjoyed my dad's music—Mr. Clarence Washington. This guy was awesome. He was a big, bald, older African-American man with a space between his two front teeth. He would shake everyone's hand while passing them a wrapped mint tucked away in his palm. And he would wear these colorful, plaid, double-breasted suits with white patent-leather saddle shoes. There were some weeks he looked like he could have been the church's pimp. During my dad's songs he would yell, "Make it plain," or "Alright," with an occasional, "Turn the lights on," for good measure.

His shouts of spiritual bliss would get other people riled up, and for a church that had the slowest hymns known to mankind and that hated any songs with a beat, my father's country music really brought the house down.

One time my father brought in some music that was originally recorded as a secular pop song but was ambiguous enough that he decided if he threw the words "church" and "God" in the lyrics, it could double as a church song. You might know it. It was originally recorded by Robert Knight in 1967 but has since been re-recorded numerous times by various different artists—the illustrious and highly sensual "Everlasting Love." I was never told why he was asked not to bring that song back in again; all I knew was that he was upset about it.

(—Maybe 'cuz it got one of the deacon's wives all horny.—)

(—Or 'cuz everyone started listening to the Gloria Estefan version.—)

(—Disco music was created by Satan and the Democrats.—)

THE BIRDS, THE BEES... AND A FEW OTHER THINGS

Nevertheless, it was clear that my father brought in a bit of a crowd whenever he sang at church, so the choir director decided that every year for the Christmas play, he should play the Angel Gabriel who told Mary about her virgin pregnancy with Jesus. Now, let me preface this next part by saying that my father had *retinitis pigmentosa*, which means he had no peripheral vision and couldn't see at all if it was even the least bit dark. So, if I wasn't paying attention to the play, I always knew when it was time for him to go on. Through dead silence and a prolonged blackout, all you'd hear was his voice in a high-pitched whisper saying, "Oh shoot," accompanied by the chorus of crashing music stands. Within seconds, he would hobble on stage and sing his big *a cappella* number. I always wondered why the Angel Gabriel held a hand microphone and sang like a lounge singer, but I was eleven so I just went with it.

That same year, I won the lead role in the school musical as Psalty, the God-fearing singing, blue songbook and got to sing a bluesy gospel version of "This Little Light of Mine" all by myself. I was pumped. I was psyched. I drank two chocolate milks everyday and warmed up my inner Stevie Wonder with a few arpeggios to adequately prepare for this once-in-a lifetime opportunity.

Two weeks before my big debut, my father caught me at home practicing in front of the bathroom mirror, singing like a young Marvin Gaye. "You're going to sing it like that?" he asked, showing a disapproving glare. "The way you're singing it sounds kind of fruity. If I were you, I'd do it more traditional; that way people will like it, and it won't stink."

In spite of my father's encouraging words, my star turn as Psalty went great, which didn't get me my dream date with Joanna Kerns, but it did help me—along with my awkward charm and burgeoning good looks—score my first church girlfriend Becky. She was tall, blonde, and had braces. She was everything I was looking for.

When my mother found out about Becky, she decided it was the perfect time to give me and my sister love advice and make it clear what relationships were all about. "Joshua, Erica, let me tell you a little story about how your father and I met," she said with very little sentiment in her voice. "It was 1977 and he came into the department store where I used to work part time. I sold him an armchair. Don't tell your father you know this, but he and I met just over ten years after his own father killed himself. It was very traumatic for him."

* * *

My paternal grandfather, Haakon Rivedal, died long before I was born and is someone whom I know very little about. But much like a slingshot, we have to stretch backward in order to gain the proper amount of momentum to propel forward with our story.

From the time I was a little boy I had a nagging curiosity about Haakon. He was a handsome Nordic, Cary Grant type whose black and white photo hung by a single thumbtack on the wall over my father's desk in his bedroom.

"Dad, Dad, tell me about the man in the picture. He's *your* dad, isn't he?" my miniature, bobble-headed six-year-old self asked my father as he sat at his desk with a furrowed brow, pretending he was busy doing whatever it is that fathers do. We had talked openly (albeit infrequently) about the lives of my three other grandparents, all of whom died of something called cancer before I was even a seed in my mommy's belly. But whenever I asked my father about Haakon, it caused him to become completely still and rendered him speechless.

"Yes that's Haakon. He was my dad," he said while shifting uncomfortably in his chair. "But I can't talk now. I need to go back to work."

"He *was* your dad. That means he's not alive anymore. What happened to him?" I asked, interrogating him like one of the great television detectives from *Law & Order*.

"I was only seventeen. He passed away from... from the shrapnel he got while serving in World War II," he said while stifling a nasty cough. "Now I have to go back to work."

You've won this round, Daddy-o. But I wasn't completely satisfied with the answers he gave. I still needed to know how and where this "World War II" occurred and why it gave my grandfather something called "shrapnel."

My ancestral fascination spurred me on to do a little sleuthing during my middle school years. I hoped whatever I dug up about Haakon would unlock some sort of mystery about myself, and cast some light on why my father was such a mercurial bastard who could so easily vacillate between benevolence and cruelty.

Once, I put together a little timeline of events to shed some light on the mystery that was Haakon, starting with the conclusion of the second World War in 1945, followed by my father's birth in 1949, and finally Haakon's death seventeen years later in 1966.

Thanks to my occasional powers of deductive reasoning, I came to the conclusion that there was no possible way Haakon died of shrapnel twenty-one years after the end of World War II. My father was not being entirely truthful, but why?

* * *

"... because he is ashamed and embarrassed about having a family member who killed himself," my mother said, continuing along in her instructional and emotionless monologue.

Holy cow, it was a suicide. I had only heard rumors about the "s" word. I never knew anyone who had actually chosen that path. Learning of my dad's shame over his father made me feel pretty icky inside.

"Promise me you won't tell your father you know about this." My mother spoke with a forbidding fear that I had never heard from her before.

"I promise," my sister and I both recited in unison.

"Can you go back to the part about how you and Dad met? Like how and why you got married," my tenderhearted sister added, hoping to segue to a more cheerful subject.

"We felt sorry for each other," my mother answered abruptly.

And that was the unfortunate conclusion to my introductory lesson on romantic relationships.

....

FOUR

A PROLOGUE PART THREE—
THE RETURN, WAIT, NO THE
ESCAPE OF THE JEDI

Middle school had now come to a close and somehow I ended up becoming the salutatorian of my eighth grade class. I was second best out of fourteen. By ninth grade, my first experience with public school, my father's verbal abuse had whittled away much of my self-confidence and left me feeling inadequate and with perpetual melancholy.

I tried to combat my father's aggression and break out of my funk by joining the freshman football team. I figured I could become equal parts star football player and acting dynamo—something of a Howie Long or Dick Butkus. Though my studly five-foot-three inch and one-hundred-and-thirty-pound frame prevented me from doing any type of damage on the field, I did have the arduous task of making sure the bench didn't get too cold during the games. After discovering I was less Dick Butkus and more Dick Van Dyke, I tried out for the school musical (not the kind of unholy pageantry put on at my church every Christmas and Easter, but in the Broadway style) and won the coveted role of Rusty Charlie, the singing streetwise gambler.

Taking part in high school theatre helped open doors to rooms filled with self-reliance, self-confidence, and a groove that would make Stella Payne jealous. I was able to make friends at school and was given the ever sexy and equally delicious nickname "White Chocolate." I even got hired to work a teenager's dream job at Six Flags Great Adventure running the roller coaster ride photos. And I was finally capable of talking to high school girls while looking them in the eyes instead of staring down at the ground.

Milk was also doing my body good, and I grew eight inches between my freshman and sophomore years—a probable contributing factor that put an end to any more beatings from my father. However, his verbal barbs did not stop and often caused my new and frail self-confidence to go into relapse.

THE SPREAD EAGLE... ER, UH... THE EAGLE SPREADS HIS WINGS

It became clear to me that if I wanted to gain true freedom, I'd need to get my very own car. Saving nearly every penny I made at Six Flags, I purchased a truly incredible jet-black 1990 Volkswagen Jetta Wolfsburg Edition, complete with gold-colored hood and a wind-up sunroof. It also featured a broken anti-theft device that wouldn't allow the car to start unless I connected two frayed wires nestled between the driver's-side door and the shoulder seatbelt strap.

I named my precious mechanical steed "The Gold Capped Tooth," and having it made me free—free to meet up with my friends whenever I wanted and free to drive to work to do double shifts on Sundays, just so I didn't have to go to church. Sometimes freedom even meant going on a date and having to push my car out of the Applebee's parking lot after dessert. But I digress.

Following my graduation from high school, "Operation Freedom" began to sputter. I lived with my parents for another year as the result of turning in my college applications too late. To keep busy and away from home I performed in a variety of community theatre shows, attended classes at a community college, and worked full time at a shoe store to pay the bills. It wasn't glamorous work, but I was helping bunion-plagued older women find comfortable sneakers, and you can't put a price on that. As I was beginning to spread my wings, my father didn't quite know what to do with me.

One Sunday afternoon prior to leaving for a rehearsal for *West Side Story* (in which I played Geetar the Jet who danced in the back of every number), my father felt the need to pull me aside for a little heart-to-heart.

"Josh, before you go, I want to say I'm happy you're working so hard, but I want to see you in church more often. You're becoming a backsliding Christian. James 2:20 says, 'Faith without works is dead,'" he said, sermonizing me in the doorway between the kitchen and the dining room.

"Yeah, but what about Romans 3:28?" I retorted. "'A person is justified by faith, not through the law.' I've got faith and I'm a good person, so I don't need to go to church five times a week."

His little eyes, each usually the size of a shrunken lima bean, grew as big as I'd ever seen them— maybe the size of *two* shrunken lima beans. He grunted. "Uh, well, then, uh... just try to get there on Sundays, then." Josh - 1. Douglas - 6,573.

That first year of college came and went with very little fanfare. I studied. I passed all of my classes except pre-calculus. More importantly, my eyes were open to the reality that the acting bug I had been infected with since childhood had now become a full-blown acting STD (my understanding of sex ed was still quite limited). So, a friend and I decided we would take a risk and quit school to ride the bus up to New York City to audition for professional shows.

Within a month I booked my first professional theatre job, cast as Willard in *Footloose* and Rolf in *The Sound of Music*. I spent that summer eight hours away from home in Lock Haven, Pennsylvania, for seven whole weeks. Shows were put on in a barn that someone so brilliantly converted to a theater. It was sweet, sweet freedom.

That summer I learned some important life lessons: Scotch is for sipping and not for chugging; if you think you might get hospitalized for alcohol poisoning, make sure you do it among friends; and women love straight men who work in theatre because there aren't very many of them. (Straight men beware. These women might demand things from you like time, money, or your virginity.)

At the end of the seven weeks, I dreaded going back home to live under the iron fist of Comrade Douglas. Luckily, in less than a week my best friend, Steve Cocowitz, who was attending Rutgers University, called me with an offer I couldn't refuse. "Hey, Josh, I'm moving out of the dorms and want to get an apartment near campus, but I need a roommate. What do you say?" I was broke, I had no job prospects, and my car had stopped working. So naturally I said, "Yes."

Look Mom, I'm On TV

New Brunswick, New Jersey, was forty-five minutes away from home. I worked like a dog—the kind that could sit, stay, and wait tables on four hours of sleep, splitting eighty hours a week between Denny's and Ruby Tuesdays just to be able to pay his rent. Nevertheless, I was thrilled to finally be on my own.

Despite winning my freedom, there was a singular giant obstacle that still got in the way of my eternal happiness: the only thing I was the star of was the Denny's night shift employee of the week contest. A co-worker from Ruby Tuesday's, Marcus, landed an internship as a costume designer for a major television network show and called me out of the blue one day from New York City.

"Josh, my producers are in a jam and need an actor for a new episode. All you have to do is come up to the city and take your shirt off for the producers of, you know, *The Maury Povich Show*.

I drove up to New York City that very same day and was hired for one of their "sexy opposites" episodes, which featured an array of different couples that ranged from moderately unusual to utterly preposterous. Among them were a voluptuous young black woman and a gaunt white cowboy more than twice her age, a little person and his abnormally tall girlfriend, and an eighty-year-old "rapping granny" and her high school-aged boyfriend. I was asked to play a white trash version of myself who was engaged to my long-distance fiancée, Kimmy, who doubled as a call girl and weighed approximately 450 pounds.

On the eve of my television premiere, Kimmy and I were required to do an on-camera interview with just the two of us. Since the producers wanted a big reveal, they didn't want to show my face in the interview. They had me say, "I love it when Kimmy rubs her hands through my hair," in my most sensual voice, while she nibbled on my ear in a close-up shot. At first it was alright, but I soon began to feel like hot meat section of the buffet at the Golden Corral.

During the actual episode, Kimmy was revealed first, dressed in a black pleather halter top with matching miniskirt and red boa. Things were spilling out everywhere. For my entrance, I was dressed in a black tank top T-shirt and black soccer shorts that came up halfway between my knee and my crotch. Gasps and long-winded swear words were coming from the audience upon seeing this thin piece of Wonder Bread make his way onto the stage to proclaim his love for an industrial-sized potato loaf. I may have become the only white dude in television history to say, "I love that Bedunkadunk."

Following the first airing of my episode, a few people recognized me in public. There were even some kids from high school that thought the show was real and posted on the Internet that "Josh Rivedal's life has suddenly gone down the toilet."

LET MY PEOPLE GO

Meanwhile, back at the Rivedal Reservation, my father continued to terrorize the natives. The position of verbal whipping post was assigned to my sister whenever my mother wasn't around. Despite her misery, Erica could never seem to devise an "Operation Freedom" of her own. Jacob grew into a taller, burlier, church-ier version of myself (think a young Ben Affleck with the fitness regimen of James Gandolfini). He escaped my father's wrath because of their mutual interest in Baptist dogma and Saturdays spent together watching repeats of Ken Burns' eleven-hour documentary *The Civil War*.

Phone calls from my mother were becoming more frequent. Her complaints often sounded like some variation of: "I've had it with your father. He's mean, he calls me names, and he's disgusting. I just want to leave, but I don't know what to do and I don't have anyplace to go." My favorite phone call was the time she complained that my father "clips his toenails and puts them in the potted plants because he thinks it helps the plants grow."

It broke my heart to see my mother and sister toiling away in Egypt while I continued on to my own promised land. I wished I could conjure my inner Moses and release them from their bondage, but the Pharaoh Doug would never let them go.

YOUNG LOVE

The summer after my move to New Brunswick, I got cast as one of the lead roles in a developmental workshop of a new musical *Hell's Kitchen*. One of my castmates, Amanda, lived in the heart of Manhattan and invited me to her birthday party late on a Saturday night. I didn't think I would get out of my restaurant job at Applebee's in time to make the party but business was slow that night and I got let go three hours earlier than usual. I decided to fill the time by taking a ninety-minute trip into Manhattan to enjoy a drunken night with Amanda and her group of friends.

When I arrived, Amanda's house party was already chock-full of hippies, Wiccans from her coven, and fellow cast members. The very first person in the room who caught my eye was a beautiful and spritely little creature with blond hair and soft blue eyes. Her smile—a thing of which clichéd love songs were made—was comprised of straight, pearly-white teeth enwrapped by two perfectly formed pink lips. She had tattoos on her chest, wrists, and, from what I could tell, her waist as well. I had never seen a woman like this before, the perfect fusion of wholesome and badass.

But Lara, this mystical creature, a life-sized pixie made of perfection, was all tied up in conversation with my friend Nick.

After a few beers and a forgettable hour of conversation with one of Amanda's eccentric hippie friends, Lara, looking to refresh her drink, finally broke free of Nick. I rushed over to the red insulated cooler that stored what was left of the cold beer.

"You look like you could use a beer," I said while pulling out two bottles of Heineken, popping open one, and handing it to her all in one seamless motion.

"Thank you," she replied with a delightful little grin as she took one of the beers from my hand.

Words that may have been small talk or the chorus of a Backstreet Boys song started involuntarily coming out of my mouth. Whatever I was saying made the corners of her lips become fixed to the bottom of her little ears.

Soon, words came out of her mouth and we moved our little tête-à-tête to the middle of the living room. For the next few hours we sat Indian-style drinking beer, talking about everything we had in common—growing up in New Jersey, going to Vacation Bible School, a fondness for the music of *Queen*, and the intricacies of our likes and dislikes within our respective worlds. She was a beautiful and refreshing oasis in the middle of a room full of theatre-folk, Wiccans, hippies, psychopaths, and theatrical-hippie-Wiccan psychopaths.

Into the early-morning hours most everyone had left the party. But Lara, me, and a few others were enjoying ourselves too much to leave and all fell asleep on the hardwood floor on top of some of Amanda's spare blankets. Somehow, I gathered the courage to lie beside Lara with my arm draped over her sleeping body—secure enough in my masculinity and the connection we had made to not try any moves (the minuscule arsenal I had) on her that night. Something in the way she moved me hinted to my twenty-year-old self that she was future wife material. Whatever action, tender satisfaction, I could get lying on that hardwood floor would probably spoil any future I may have had with this girl.

The next morning, I walked her out of the apartment and down to the street corner where I boldly leaned my head in to kiss her on the mouth. My move caught her completely by surprise, but not to the point where she didn't kiss me back.

"I had a really nice time talking to you. Hopefully I'll see you soon," I said with the pangs of love, blue balls, and a mild hangover pulsing through my body.

"Okay," was all she said.

Usually painfully shy with women, I had a fresh swagger about myself while on the train back to New Jersey.

(—*Playa, playa! Do your pimp walk. Won't stop, can't...*—)

(—Stop it. I'm not a bad boy and she's cool.—)

(—*But whosoever looketh on a woman to lust after...*—)

(—Shit! I forgot to get her phone number.—)

(—*Relax, dumbass. Just get her number from her homegirl, Amanda.*—)

I *had* to wait a few weeks to call her. The last thing I wanted to do was come on too strong. Asinine advice from an article I had read in *Seventeen* magazine—a sad page in the annals of history where socially awkward young men could have their burning questions answered about the female species without actually having to talk to them.

When we finally did connect, it was over a light dinner in New York City with mutual friends. That night ended with another surprise kiss and a long trip back to New Jersey with voices who were getting impatient with me, now suffering from their own case of blue balls. Later that same week we began talking over the phone for hours every night. In the coming weeks, nightly phone calls were replaced by entire days full of text messaging. I was even making weekly trips into Manhattan to visit her, if only for a few hours at a time.

A month into our courtship, I took a bit of a risk. "I'm in love with you," I said while summoning every piece of self-confidence that lived in my body—from the little hairs on the back of my neck, all the way to that forgotten bit in my left pinky toe. I was only twenty years old, but she was twenty-three and much more worldly than I. It seemed as if my impetuous declaration caught her off guard by the quizzical look she gave me. But when she realized that I meant what I said, her puzzled look melted into a half smile. "I'm—I'm *beginning* to fall in love with you too," she said, an answer that was more than good enough for me.

Later in the summer, Lara visited me in New Jersey for the very first time for a day trip. At some point that evening I found a backbone and asked her to stay the night with me in the musty basement of my apartment that doubled as my bedroom—and she said yes. From that point on our love was mutual and official, it was beautiful, and nothing like I had ever known.

TOILING AT BREAK-EVEN

Within six months I moved to the Big Apple to live with Lara in her apartment full time, much to the chagrin of my father.

"You need to marry that girl right now, Joshua," my father demanded. "Somebody needs to tell that girl not to cast her pearls before swine."

"I'm sorry, Dad, I can't understand you with all that oinking coming out of your mouth," I said.

With a beautiful blonde-haired girlfriend, a Manhattan apartment, and some initial career success, I had essentially accomplished my childhood dream. This should have been my "happily ever after," but none of it gave me any real satisfaction and I couldn't figure out why. I reached the end of the proverbial rainbow, but instead of a huge pot of gold, all I found was an unquenchable feeling of emptiness. What would life bring next? Was I supposed to go further or complete some kind of magic formula? Maybe if got on Broadway or did films I'd be happier and my life would mean something. The harder I pressed, the worse I felt, and to top it all off I suddenly stopped booking acting jobs.

The only work I could get for three years was in a high-end seafood restaurant as a food runner. I was the guy who brought out the meal and then described what it was with the detail and intricacy of an epic catalogue:

"Sing to me, oh Muse, the fruits of the sea!
Blue Point Oysters from Long Island, New York.
Here we have Wellfleets from Massachusetts.
These little fellows are Kumamotos,
They're from Washington State. Oh, my goodness!
And the Hama Hamas over here, *wow*,
Delish, they're from Washington State as well.
Here we have a cocktail sauce, some lemons...

This here is a Thai mignonette, spicy.
Here is a red Wine mignonette, quite tart.
Everything here is gluten free, dairy free,
Peanut free, and kosher free. Just kidding.
That's a bit of Levitical humor.
Enjoy everyone. Ciao. Bon appétit."

If I wanted to scare anyone, the oysters on the right were from the East River off the coast of Manhattan and the oysters on the left were from the Gulf Coast. The milky looking black stuff inside the shell was just oil that needed a light rinsing off.

The longer I toiled at financial break-even with a mediocre-paying restaurant job and without acting work, the more those little voices in my head began to nag me.

(—*Hey, bitch, way to leave home to become a professional waiter.*—)

(—*Sí, papi. You should've done something that actually pays, an abogado.* —)

(—*Not a lawyer, a preacher. Though a moral compass would be needed for that.*—)

The faster my dreams of Broadway and Hollywood circled the drain, the harder I swam against the current until most of my waking hours were spent simply trying to figure out how to keep my head above water. This left little time for anything else, much less Lara. I loved her, but it was impossible to serve two masters.

"Josh, I feel like I only ever see you in passing. We need to make time for each other more often. We need to get away for a weekend," she said, her eyes pleading for the slightest bit of compromise.

"Babe, I would love to. But it's hard to get off from the restaurant... and it's audition season right now. Maybe we can do something in a few months," I said while her face turned to a deep shade of disappointment.

Right as my romantic relationship began developing some razor-thin cracks, my parents' marriage shattered completely. The dissolution of their marital relationship came to a head in late August 2008 when my mother called me one morning sounding like she was rabid and foaming at the mouth.

"I did it, Joshua. I did it. I did it. I did it. I did it."

"Did what?" I asked. "What are you talking about?"

"I moved out. I left your father." She sounded both relieved and petrified.

"Holy cow. What did he do? What did he say? Are you okay? You're not hurt, are you?" I asked, afraid that his famous temper boiled over into the realm of domestic violence, burning my mother.

"No, he doesn't know yet. He'll find out when he gets home from work tonight. I've had to plan this in secret for months. You know how angry your father gets."

"I do. Just make sure you call me tonight after he finds out."

My father took the news of getting dumped worse than any of us expected. Instead of blowing up and trashing the house, he withered up and became a shell of his former self. He stopped going to work every day and only attended church once in a while. He started calling me at odd times of the day just to talk, and it was almost always about my mother. Occasionally he would ask me about my problems and actually gave thoughtful responses—something he never took the time to do when I was a child.

We were developing something that resembled a friendship, something I had always wanted from him. But the timing of his new attention to our relationship made me furious because it felt like it was only a force of circumstance. At the same time that the world economy was collapsing, so was my father's life. He, unlike a select few, was nowhere near being too big to fail and had no one to bail him out... except me.

One morning in early March, just before an afternoon shift at my restaurant job, I got a call from my father.

"Josh, Josh I just don't understand your mother. I know we've had our problems, but it's not all my fault," he said. His voice weighed heavily with desperation. It was exactly one month prior to the completion of their divorce. "I don't know what I'll do if she goes through with this."

"There's always a chance you guys can work things out even if you get divorced. It's just a piece of paper," I said, offering him the chance to borrow my limited edition rose-colored glasses.

"I don't know. I have nothing in this world if I don't have my wife."

"That is not true, man. But listen, I have to get in to work."

"No problem, Josh. Whatever happens, I want you to know that I love you and I'm proud of you." Click.

FIVE

THE FAMILY HEIRLOOM

It was late afternoon on March 31, 2009, a Tuesday, and I was having lunch with my friend David at a colorful little Thai restaurant in the Broadway district in New York City. David and I had done a production of Elton John's *Aida* at The Media Theatre, just outside of Philadelphia, and we were reconnecting on account of having lost touch for about a year and a half.

David, a dignified, pseudo-hippie, gay, black man more than twice my age, was a rare soul with whom I had a lot in common. Besides theatre, we both loved crossword puzzles, had a distaste for our oppressive religious upbringings, and had a mutual interest in the horticulture of cannabis and its effects on the human cerebral matter—specifically our own.

By the time we sat down and our appetizers delivered, my pants pocket had vibrated five separate times with phone calls from my mother—a little ominous because her calls had dwindled to once a month to complain about my father or to spill the beans on some juicy church gossip. I was hedging my bets that someone drowned in the baptismal, the preacher got someone pregnant, or my father showed up at her job to harass her. Whatever it was, short of nuclear war breaking out, it would have to wait. There's nothing worse than an angry lunch partner and cold Thai food (maybe cold Indian food), so I shut my phone off in time for the delivery of our main courses and effectively silenced my mother.

After wrapping up lunch and a deep conversation about magic brownies, I hustled out of the restaurant, sent David on his way, and dug through the front right pocket of my jeans. A notification of ten new voicemails popped up on the screen followed by a text message from my mother:

-JOSH YOU NEED TO CALL ME BACK AS SOON AS POSSIBLE. THIS IS AN EMERGENCY.

And here I was hoping that one of the deacons had embezzled money from the church. Nausea set in and my mind began to race.

(—Maybe she was in a terrible car accident.—)
(—*At least she still has her thumbs, homeboy.*—)
(—Maybe the house burned down.—)
(—*She doesn't live there anymore, papi chulo.*—)
(—This is about my dad. It's gotta be him.—)
(—*The Lord giveth, the Lord taketh away...*—)

A CRUMBLING DICTATORSHIP

In the seven months since my mother left him, his Darth Vader-like persona had morphed into that of an Eeyore. Even so, I knew that within him still lived a man with a dark side that bordered on self-destructive, an odious beast who could put the Artist-Formerly-Known-as-Anakin to shame.

Earlier in the year he confided in me that he had recently started taking prescription pills to help him sleep—this from a man who had the sleeping habits of a grizzly bear in the dead of winter and who hated ingesting medicine of any kind. The last time I'd seen him was for his birthday back in January. I took the train down from New York and when I arrived, the first thing I noticed was that his skin had a light yellow complexion and was sagging off of his face. He looked like the love child of Tweety Bird and Droopy the cartoon dog. From what I could tell, he hadn't been eating much—a shocking change for someone who weighed a portly two hundred and fifty pounds for most of his adult life and counted cupcakes, fast food, and bacon as three of his major food groups.

"Happy birthday, buddy boy—the big six-oh," I said while smothering him with a bear hug. "What do you want to do today, huh? Should we go blow your first social security check? We can do anything you want!"

"I was actually hoping you would help me cut some firewood and maybe, I don't know, you could talk to me about your mother. She has stopped returning my calls."

Of course she stopped returning his calls. They were legally separated and he was still calling her three times a day. Plus he was about as fun to be around as a root canal. Some people jump out of planes with their sons on their sixtieth birthday, but I had to listen to him whine about my mother while I cut down a few trees for firewood because he tore both of his rotator cuffs.

Frankly, I was surprised he was still holding a candle to the memory of his marriage. I was always under the impression he was either a misogynist or that he truly hated my mother. All of those euphemistic names for stupid, fat, and ugly he used to call her didn't matter anymore. My father just wanted his woman back—for better or for worse.

During this sixtieth birthday visit, the only time he showed any sort of excitement (and the only time his skin color appeared to be human) was during our drive from the train station and back to his house. "I have every right to be angry about what your mother has done to me," he said, keeping his eyes firmly fixed on the road in front of him while waving his right hand in the air for emphasis.

"And why is that? Why do you get to be angry about this?" I asked, wondering what kind of nonsense was about to spew out of his mouth next.

"She was a terrible homemaker. She never cleaned anything properly and she was too shy. Your mother has this great busty body and she would hide it and never wanted to give of herself, her breasts—"

"Whoa, whoa, and this is where I have to stop you. This is the part I *don't* want to hear about," I said in terror and disgust.

"Well, don't ask if you don't want to know," he said, growling back at me.

Here's some free advice*—(*This is neither free nor actual advice)—if you're ever driving anywhere with your father and he starts to talk about your mother's breasts, don't be afraid to give him a little backhanded slap to the face, something I should have done. The pain he'll feel is a lot better than the kind you'll suffer upon hearing your father use the words "breasts" and "your mother" in the same sentence.

While struggling to remove from my mind the heinous picture of my parents having uncomfortable and awkward sex, my father went on to describe how he was going to trick my mother into meeting him at a local Dunkin' Donuts. While there he would remind her that she would be giving up her spot in heaven if she dared to go through with the divorce (not exactly Romeo and Juliet material or that John Cusack boom box thing in *Say Anything,* but somehow in his head it worked).

As I listened to him wax idiotic about the perfection of his strategy, I knew there was no way that she'd ever let him fool her with his secret little plan. She hated coffee. And from our confidential conversations, she had told me she was done with my father. But there was no way I was going to tell him any of that on his birthday. If I did, he probably would've run the car off the road with me still inside.

FILLING HIS FATHER'S SHOES

The pieces of this morbid puzzle were all coming together as I looked down at my phone, still blinking with ten voicemails and an urgent text message from my mother. I called her straightaway. She picked up halfway through the first ring.

"Hi, Josh," she said. Her voice was dark and solemn like I was expecting. At least she wasn't dead.

"Hi. What's up?" I replied anxiously. "I didn't check my voicemail."

"Oh..." she said, letting out a long sigh. "Listen, there were paramedics at your father's house this morning. It looks like he... well, he killed himself. He's dead. I am so sorry Josh."

I was waiting to hear "April Fools." There was still a slim chance that my mother had forgotten there were thirty-one days in March and was making a terrible attempt at some sort of inappropriate practical joke. But the punch line never came. This was real. But what is someone supposed to do or say when their parent kills himself? Is there a detailed instruction manual for this somewhere? If so, I hope it also explains what to do if you don't like that dead parent very much.

Fighting for both oxygen and the ability to speak, I began to mourn for what could have been. Despite my lifetime of contempt for him, I had always held out hope that he would become the father I had always wanted—a man whom I could go to for advice, confide in, and trust. Now that things between the two of us had started to improve, he threw it all away, leaving me wanting more.

As I regained the capacity to form words, my pragmatic mind went into overdrive.

"Listen, we've got to figure out the funeral arrangements. When and where..."

"We're going to have the service this Saturday at the church," she said in a hushed, staccato tenor.

"Okay. How are Jacob and Erica doing? How are you doing? You know this is nobody's fault. I mean, this is totally on him—not us."

"I know. Everyone's just upset. I just can't believe he left you kids without a father, after his own father did this to him. It's a shame. I'm sorry, Josh," she said. Her voice cracked as she said my name.

Was she sorry for me? Did she blame herself? Did she love this man in spite of all his glaring faults?

"Yeah... um," was all I could think to say, my voice finally quivering. "I guess I'll come down tonight and see how I can help. I don't know."

"That would be good. We are going to have to go through your father's stuff and get the house ready to sell," she said, keeping the conversation a practical one.

"Of course."

"Listen, I have to go now and make a few other calls, but I love you, Josh."

"I love you too. I'll see you soon."

He was only sixty, a young sixty, and he shouldn't have been dead. Suddenly, a feeling I didn't expect would come so soon rose to the surface and reared its ugly head. This monster's name was Relief.

(—*You ain't never gonna have to deal with this asshole again, dawg.*—)

(—How dare you?—)

(—*Coño, he's never going to hurt you again.*—)

(—*No! Honor thy father. You must give penance for these evil thoughts.*—)

(—I can't. People are watching.—)

(—*Twenty self-flagellating blows to the head. Peace be with you.*—)

Hidden in an alleyway, smacking myself in the head, was not making my pain go away. The only other comfort I could find was inside the half-pack of menthol cigarettes from the interior pocket of my coat. Both of my hands shook violently as I put a cigarette to my lips. As I took my first puff, the smoke displaced the oxygen in my brain. Each inhale followed by an exhale provided me with a temporary high that helped propel my body forward through the Broadway district and toward my apartment on the Upper East Side of Manhattan. Tears were flowing down my face and into my mouth. They mixed with the cigarette smoke, forming a kind of cocktail whose recipe included a splash of saline and equal parts misery, nicotine, and carbon monoxide.

As I chain-smoked my way through crowds of foreign tourists and business professionals, a little redheaded girl, no more than five years old, walked toward me with an orange balloon tied to her finger while holding her father's hand. My sister Erica had recently made amends with my father, despite a lifetime of his verbal abuse. She was getting married next year to her boyfriend of four years, Joe, and had asked my father to give her away. His suicide directly affected those plans and I needed to call her to make sure she was okay. My call went straight to voicemail.

"Hey, um, I didn't want to leave a message, but... I'm sorry about Dad... and all of this. And I just want to let you know, I'll walk you down the aisle next year. I'll step up for Dad... if you want. I'll see you tomorrow."

I had spent my whole life playing understudy to my father, offering advice and reassurance to my brother, giving love and support to my sister and mother that my father refused to provide. I was always cleaning up the messes he made with me and the rest of my family. But the star of our show, this long-running familial soap opera, was never coming back and it was time for me to assume the lead role indefinitely.

One of the benefits of living with someone who is far from your ideal role model is the invaluable educational experience of learning not to do things like: throw temper tantrums when you're arguing with people, tell your female friends that "they're putting on a few pounds," or bottle up your emotions till they become toxic and fermented, like when a family member kills himself.

On my walk home I decided I'd have to start talking about that very same "S" word my father had been running from his entire adult life—*suicide*. But how exactly do you tell someone that your father just killed himself? What does *that* phone call sound like? Thinking about it was giving me mild chest pains, which also could have been a product of the chilies from the Thai food. Suicide is just not something that people talk about. Religion and politics, those very famous taboo water cooler topics, ain't got nothin' on suicide, the red-headed stepchild of conversationalists everywhere.

Still more than thirty blocks away from my apartment, my first call was to Lara, who was still at her hotel accounting job crunching numbers.

"Hey, it's me," I said.

"Hey there. What's up?" she asked, surprised that I was calling her toward the end of her workday.

"Not too much," I replied. I didn't yet have the courage to reveal the truth. That my asshole of a father just killed himself and all I wanted was to scream, to be hugged, and then left alone.

"I'm a little busy. I can't talk long," she said, seemingly irritated that I was calling her for no particular reason. My interruption threatened to keep her on the job longer than a normal eight-hour work day.

"No, it's cool... um, so my father just died," I said, choking on my words.

"Oh my gosh, Josh. How did this happen? Are you okay?" she asked. Her voice became soft and faint as if it was floating away.

"Yeah, well, they think he killed himself... a suicide... but they're not sure."

"Oh... oh, my gosh," she said. Her initial shock at hearing the word "suicide" was greater than mine, probably because she didn't know my father as well I did. "I'm so sorry, Josh. I... I'm going to leave right now. I'm coming home."

"That would be awesome. But actually, can you give me an hour? I just need a little time. I love you."

That didn't go nearly as bad as I'd imagined. The sound of the word "suicide" didn't cause any weeping and gnashing of teeth like from the Book of Revelation or projectile vomiting like from *The Exorcist*.

And talking about the "S" word with her, actually saying the word, had helped clear away the carbon monoxide clouds and pump some much-needed oxygen back into my brain. In my lucid state, I realized I needed to call those few trusted friends from my churchgoing days in advance of the ecclesiastical gossip train's arrival with news about my father's death.

The first three calls I made all rung through to voicemail. I left messages to each about a suicide in the Rivedal family. Condolences from these three friends from my youth were not returned for at least a few weeks. To paraphrase Rodney Dangerfield—redheaded stepchildren don't get no regard.

The fourth call I made was to my friend Ryan who also happened to like redheads, and just about any other species of woman that was older than seventeen and could walk (bless his heart). He and I had been friends since grade school. We grew up in the same church and both raged against the pious pastoral machine from puberty through adulthood. During Sunday church services we'd sit on the balcony above the rest of the congregation so we could get the best view for making fun of all the people who had silly voices, wore stupid hats, or were just plain weird looking. We were a young, stringless version of the Statler & Waldorf Muppet team.

Ryan and I casually maintained our friendship throughout high school and college, often comparing notes on the new swear words we learned, the beers we drank, and the girls we slept with. That probably doesn't sound like a big deal, but where I come from people treat you like a serial rapist if you're caught at the local Barnes & Noble thumbing through the *Sports Illustrated* Swimsuit Edition (the soft-core eroticism of the 1998 Heidi Klum cover got my horny and pimpled-fourteen year-old self into some hard-core trouble).

Ryan picked up the phone immediately and listened to everything I had to say. There was no judgment when he spoke, only empathy and assurance. He promised to attend my father's funeral services wherever and whenever they were taking place.

As I finished my conversation with him, the blinders of concentration now removed, I was surprised to find myself across the street from the dilapidated vacant Chinese restaurant in my neighborhood. I had walked nearly fifty blocks over the course of two hours. I approached my apartment building unsteady on my feet. I was dreading going inside. Eventually I'd have to face my girlfriend, and seeing her would make my father's death an actuality. I forced my key into each of the two doors that stood guard over the tenants of my building from the outside world, and then dragged my feet up every step of that five-floor walkup.

Inside my apartment, I pulled close all of the curtains and waited for Lara in the dark for almost fifteen minutes before the lock on the front door started to move. I jumped up and met her at the door. Her face was drenched in tears.

"Hey," she said, standing in the doorway.

"Hey," I replied while keeping my distance in the shadows.

I stood there completely still. The singular thought that I did not want him to be dead clattered around in my head like a pit of rattlesnakes, fit to be tied. The sound was almost deafening.

Lara dropped her things at the door, came inside, and held me where I stood. Her little arms fit around my waist. Her hands cupped my shoulder blades while my left arm wrapped around her right shoulder and over her back. My right hand cradled her head, and my head was tucked between her neck and collarbone. I then picked her up and we moved to the main room in our studio apartment and sat on our tattered beige love seat.

"I'm just so fucking disappointed... and angry that I'd expect anything less from this guy. What a shit head," I said with contempt in my voice and the beginnings of tear formations in my eyes.

"I'm so sorry, baby. I know he's your father. I just can't even imagine," she whispered, doing her best to console me.

"Thanks, I... um... I have to use the bathroom," I said, excusing myself to a place where I could cry without her seeing me.

I'm sure she knew what I was doing, but I felt like I had to look like I was strong for her because the rest of my life wasn't so solid.

Worn out from all the walking, crying, hugging, and cigarette smoking that afternoon, I let my mother know that a trip to New Jersey would have to wait till tomorrow morning.

The best thing for me to do was to stay in my shoebox-sized apartment, and order in some comforting soul food from the barbecue restaurant around the corner. That night, I found solace in the arms of BBQ ribs, macaroni & cheese, collard greens, fried zucchini, and a six-pack of beer.

I went to bed that night lying next to Lara, looking up at the ceiling with the room spinning around me, brooding over Douglas and my own mortality and existence on this planet. I was reminded about my own flirtation with self-death as a bruised and broken eleven-year-old boy.

I fell asleep that night, half-drunk and bloated from barbecue sauce and roasted pork, wondering if someday I was destined to inherit the family legacy that my father had left behind.

SIX

....

TODAY IS THE FIRST DAY OF
THE REST OF YOUR LIFE
(FACE-PALM)

At what moment does the "first day of the rest of your life" actually begin? Whoever came up with that phrase should get punched in the kidney for such an obnoxious and cliché attempt to inspire their fellow human beings.

The morning of April 1st, after shaking off a mild hangover and a soul food-induced coma, I traveled to New Jersey to meet my brother, sister, and mother at my father's house. The first thing we did was look for a note. Maybe there was still hope— hope that Douglas wrote us a letter explaining himself, or hope that there was no note and this was just some big silly accident. So, we tore my father's house apart.

We started with the kitchen—a place where his culinary skills, more idiot and less savant, lent themselves to innovations like omelets made of flaxseed, Worcestershire sauce, and kidney beans and his version of an alcohol-free champagne made of Diet Coke and grape juice.

The dining room, where he played hours of Solitaire on the family computer every night, had no sign of a note.

The bathroom was business as usual—the red book of Children's Bible stories and the blue book of Popular Judaica both sat on the heater adjacent to the toilet, their home since I was a teenager.

The living room with the natty, forest green carpet, where I spent evenings sitting on the floor in front of the television watching whatever came in on the bunny ear antennae, had no trace of a suicide note.

We searched in every nook inside that house, except for his bedroom, because nobody wanted to go in there.

But now we had no choice.

As the newly self-appointed man of the house, I volunteered to go in first. And so, I turned the knob very slowly and opened the door. I'll never forget what I saw when I went inside. The shades were drawn and the room was well lit; the window was left open by the paramedics the day prior; the ceiling fan was left on to reduce the stench that was lingering in the room; there was blood soaked into the carpet at the foot of his bed; and there, on the dresser, was the note that we were all looking for:

I'M SORRY I HAD NO CHOICE BUT TO DO THIS DUE TO THE CIRCUMSTANCES OF MY DIVORCE. TO MY CHILDREN, THE KOZLOWSKI, AND OBERTO FAMILIES I LEAVE ALL OF MY WORLDLY POSSESSIONS TO BE DIVIDED EQUALLY IN SIXTHS.
    -DOUG

That was it. Two nondescript sentences, two commas, an apostrophe, and two periods.

He could have at least painted a better picture about how he was feeling—maybe a PowerPoint presentation with some pictures and graphs or even a card made of construction paper with finger paint on it—*something* creative. Did he hate us? Did he love us?

Holding that note in my hand for the first time, I made a silent promise to myself that I'd do everything in my control to avoid the same fate as my father—an unhappy and unfulfilled life.

After the note was passed between the four of us, my mother found an empty bottle of sleeping pills wrapped between her dead, almost ex-husband's bloody bed sheets.

"He must have wanted it to be painless—to sleep through death," she expounded, coolly putting her diagnostic stamp on the situation. She could have been right or he could have been a complete moron over the whole thing. Some weeks later we found out that the overdose of sleeping pills caused his internal organs to explode, and that the painless death he may or may not have been hoping for had turned into the worst kind of agony he could have ever imagined.

Everyone filed out of my father's bedroom except me. All I could do was stand in the doorway, looking at the drafty room with his blood all over the floor, while a tingling of anger and sadness slithered up the back of my neck and pulsated through my ears and my eyes. I went into his closet, got out a dull Exact-o knife, and began to struggle trying to rip out the bloodstained parts of the carpet.

Within a few minutes, Erica peered back into the room and saw that I was having a difficult time. She returned with two knives much sharper than mine and helped me finish the job. "Thanks. You take care of that end and I'll do this end," I said, pointing to the expanse of tainted flooring.

"Sure thing. And we will meet in the middle," she replied.

We remained silent for almost a half hour until the floor looked like a spotless piece of Swiss cheese.

I would've gladly traded the opportunity to change my future ninety-year-old father's diaper or a swipe out of his colostomy bag instead of the cleanup of his messy suicide.

ADVENTURES IN FUNERAL HOME LAND

Following a few more hours of rifling through old papers, cleaning out closets, and hauling his blood-stained mattress to the curb, we all decided that we needed to get out of that house and take a field trip to the only place that seemed appropriate in a time like this—the funeral home. A place that has effectively shattered McDonald's one billion customers served, with a sizable menu that includes ten-thousand-dollar coffins, hundred-dollar prayer card packages, and a similar post-meal effect that leaves you feeling bloated and sluggish. Who knew suicide had a twenty-five-thousand-dollar price tag, roughly the cost of a new Chevy Camaro. Too bad Douglas didn't come with bucket seats and a cool racing stripe.

Our appointed funeral director, Cindi, was a handsome, square-jawed woman in her mid-forties who spelled her name with an "i," presumably to shave ten years off of her age. Sitting with her for five minutes, it became clear to me that the funeral industry employs some of the smartest people in the world.

First, they chose a profession that boasts tremendous job security thanks to the death of everyone who's ever lived. (Well, except a long-haired gentleman by the name of Jesus Christ. The funeral industry is still reeling from that little resurrection stunt he pulled.) And secondly, funeral directors are brilliant psychologists. Also known as "Death's Carpetbaggers," these wily opportunists use a combination of the Dark Side of the Force and Pavlovian psychology to elicit blind and undying reverence to your predeceased. They work to get you to concentrate solely on the good things about the dead person so you don't lose your mind when they slap that ginormous sticker price on the whole shebang because, really, nothing is too good for the vehemently racist and career criminal Grandpa Billy Joe. If he wants to meet St. Peter at the Pearly Gates in a diamond studded Robert E. Lee memorial coffin, then by golly, that is what Grandpa Billy Joe will get. He deserves it and, hell, he always put food on the table and tithed from every bank robbery.

After running through our many options, Cindi exited the doleful room, colored in five shades of sienna, while my three living family members and I sat in a circle around a conference table to discuss whether our newly canonized and saintly patriarch was going to get the gold or deluxe package.

Cindi's Jedi mind tricks had no effect on us, except for my brother Jacob—the only person in the world who's ever grown and cultivated his own money tree.

"We should bury him next to his mother in Trenton. Price is no object here," Jacob jumped right in.

"Do you have twenty-five thousand dollars for this guy?" I asked, my sarcasm cutting through the room like a dull butter knife.

"Okay, Josh, I don't think any of us are in that kind of a financial position," my mother chimed in.

"He's still our father. Now let's pass around the coffin catalogue," Erica said, playing the role of peacemaker while thumbing through the binder of fresh death-boxes for sale.

"I just don't think we owe him this. He wasn't a nice person and he really screwed us over with this," I said.

"Well, we've got to come up with something. His body can't stay here, and it's not coming back with us," my mother said with a slight chuckle.

She was right. We had to craft some sort of plan to dispose of Douglas Stewart Rivedal and do it in a way that made everybody happy. Erica touted a super saver funeral with only family and close friends. Jacob wanted to make sure Douglas met Jesus looking his very best. I made it clear I couldn't have cared less if he met Jesus wearing a burlap potato sack and offered cremation as our best way to go.

"Here's an option," my mother said, pointing at the coffin catalogue. "We can fold him in half and stuff him in this baby coffin," the thought of which caused us all to keel over in our seats with laughter.

But laughter quickly turned to prolonged bickering, an old family standby, as each of us struggled to come to terms with our grief and the final plans we had to make for our newly deposed tyrant. The roundtable democratic decision-making process wasn't working, so I temporarily assumed Douglas's former role of dictator, "Caesar Rivedalus."

"Stop it. Everyone just—stop for a minute," I said while pounding the table with both of my fists. "We're supposed to be a family, but we're not acting like it. We don't call. We don't visit. And now, we're fighting each other when, I DON'T KNOW... I don't know why he's dead, but we have to make this mean something. We have to come together. We really need to put cremation back on the table. We don't have the funds for anything else right now. He doesn't deserve a big fancy funeral— suicide or not. The guy was a jerk."

"But what will the people at church say?" my mother asked, worried about the backlash from some of the church congregation's amateur theologians.

"There's nothing in the Bible about cremation. Tell them he's still going to get raptured. And if they've got a problem with it, you can send 'em to me."

Here's a fun fact: If you're having an argument with a Christian on the fanatical side and you're getting nowhere, reinforce your position with a light Biblical reference and you'll shut them down faster than you can say, "Jesus wept" (the shortest verse in the entire Bible).

After turning over my emergency powers of autocracy, we finally agreed as a family to cremate my father, at a price tag of *only* four thousand dollars. I would have gladly incinerated his body out back for a crisp hundred-dollar bill and a gift certificate to The Cheesecake Factory but was told that to do so would be unethical, not to mention a biohazard. However, our agreement had one stinky little piece of pork barrel legislation that snuck its way into the bill—my mother preferred we not let anyone at church except the pastors know that my father's death was a suicide. She was afraid people might gossip and blame her or even us, his children, for his self-destructive final act.

It seemed silly not to tell the truth, and not exactly my ideal compromise, but it kept my family from filing bankruptcy.

I spent the train ride back to New York City that evening racking my brain for what I would tell people at my father's memorial service when they asked how he died. My Letterman list of Top Ten Causes of Death included:

- Heart attack
- Terminal gonorrhea
- Exploding diarrhea
- Nazi henchmen
- In your arms tonight
- A Cyclops
- A botched manicure
- Run over by a wheelchair
- An ACME anvil

A CRUSHING BLOW FROM BEYOND THE GRAVE

The following morning while lying in bed, unable to sleep and counting down the seconds in between one snooze alarm and the next, I received a phone call that forced me to haul myself out of bed. It was the director of a small independent feature film that I had auditioned for a month before my father's death. He wanted me to play the lead role, which was also a paid gig (a detail of tremendous importance since much of show business asks actors to work for free), and promised that the film, upon completion, would be entered into the Cannes, Tribeca, and Sundance Film Festivals.

Having not worked as an actor for more than a year and hearing him mention the holy triumvirate of film festivals, I eagerly accepted his offer hoping this would be the quantum job that would leap me to a state of frequent artistic employment. We exchanged a few pleasantries and while saying goodbye, he interrupted himself. "I'm so sorry," he said with a sheepish little laugh. "It's late notice, but we need to begin rehearsals this Saturday. Principal photography will begin the following Monday in upstate New York."

(—*Shit, son. What is you going to do about this?*—)
(—I don't know. I want to take this job... but...—)
(—*Su padre screwed you over your entire life. Now it's your turn, hijo.*—)
(—But my mom... and Jacob and Erica...—)

(—*Vengeance is mine, I will repay, says the Lord. Get thee to a funeral...*—)

"Um, actually my father just died and his memorial service is this Saturday. And, um, I just have a lot of family stuff. Is it possible to move the shoot back maybe, like two weeks?" I asked with trepidation in my voice. I hoped he would show some sympathy (you can't really turn down a guy whose father just died; that's like hitting someone in the face who's wearing glasses).

"Hey, man, I get it. But the location and crew schedule have already been set. And I'm sorry about all that with your dad," he said with an air of nonchalance, "but we're just going to have to go with our second choice here."

"No, it's cool. Thanks for considering me," I said, shrugging him off, doing my best to hide the rage and resentment brewing within.

Goodbye film director. Goodbye Cannes. Goodbye Tribeca. Goodbye Sundance. Goodbye douche bag father who wasn't considerate enough to think of a more convenient time of year to kill himself.

THE FUNERAL MARCH

Saturday, the day of my father's memorial service, was the *piece de resistance* of the flaming pile of garbage that became my week. It started at the church with a somber conga line of my father's co-workers, family friends, and church people who couldn't wait to tell me things I never knew about my father.

"We always had the most interesting conversations at work," stammered Jeffrey, one of my father's co-workers. I could barely understand him through the Kleenex that was wiping his nose and eyes in one fluid motion.

"Your dad used to make special trips just to pick me up and take me to church," said one elderly woman as she grabbed both of my hands.

"I'm sorry he and I lost touch and I'm sorry to see him go. He was a good friend for a long time," said one rosy-cheeked, potbellied gentleman with graying hair who appeared to be in his fifties.

Where was this charming man during my childhood? These people got the best of him for twenty-five years while all I got were the stale leftovers.

The church's pastor, a man who was as round as he was tall, started off the service with a solemn prayer asking God that His will be done. He followed that by leading the congregation of mourners in song with a rousing rendition of the Spafford & Bliss hymn, *It is Well With My Soul.*

"And now Joshua, Doug's oldest son, will say a few words on behalf of the family," he said as I rose from my front row seat and walked up to the podium wearing a long face and a mustard colored suit

"Thank you all for being here today. We, as a family, appreciate your love. You know, it's times like this that you see the importance of having a family and a support system," I said as my voice began to crack. "I... I want to challenge all of you here today—all you mothers, fathers, sons, granddaughters—if you're going through anything in your life that seems too tough to bear and you don't know where to turn, bring it to your family. No matter what you tell them or how strained your relationship, your family wants to help you and they love you. Families, come together today and support one another like Jesus supports you. Thank you again."

I couldn't believe the part about Jesus came out of my mouth, but the first rule of thumb for public speaking *is* to know your audience.

The preacher wrapped up the morning with a brief eulogy and a plea to all non-believers to, "turn your lives to *Jeeee*-sus. Accept Him as your Lord and Savior as Doug had once done." I didn't really see how my father could be a ringing endorsement to go running into the arms of Jesus. But then again, that radical Jewish hippie carpenter did hang out with just about anyone including tax collectors, Samaritans, members of U.S. Congress, and strippers who were only trying to pay their way through grad school.

Following the conclusion of the funerary festivities, I dashed out to grab a drink of water from the fountain in the vestibule and got cornered by a long-time church member who, for legal purposes, we'll call "Chief-Crazy-Eyed-Short-Middle-Aged-Former-Frat-Boy-Guido-Who-Walks-With-a-Cane," or "Crazy Eyes" for short.

"Josh, Josh, it's good to see you after all these years. Your dad was so young. How did he die?"

"Well..."

"Was it a heart attack?" he asked, much like a little child on Christmas morning who couldn't wait to find out what was inside of the wrapped boxes underneath the tree. "It must have been a heart attack. I have never heard of anyone dying so suddenly unless it was a heart attack."

(—*My bad, brother Crazy Eyes. I didn't know they taught medical diagnoses...*—)

(—*...at the school where you learned how to tar and shingle a roof.*—)

(—*Sí, y sudden infant death syndrome and suicides don't exist?*—)

(—*You, sir, are truly an ignorant, New Jersey hick.*—)

"Why are you just standing there with your mouth open? What was it, Josh? I'm right aren't I?"

I didn't know what to say. If I told him the truth he would probably ask me a bunch of stupid questions, which would have pissed me off even further, causing me to run off with his cane after beating him with it. A lie seemed better than jail time.

"Yes, sir, he died of a heart attack," I said through gritted teeth. "Now if you'll excuse me, I have to go back inside."

I took a deep breath and reentered the auditorium, acutely aware that it was time to graciously say goodbye to another conga line of well-wishers, and took my place alongside my sister and brother.

I headed back to New York City that evening, emotionally exhausted and grateful that I had made it through the day. But what would tomorrow bring? How was I going to feel, and what was I supposed to do with my life? Was my father's death going to be some kind of victory for the greater good of my family or simply the waste of what could have been something incredible?

There were so many unanswered questions, and in only a matter of days I would find out that picking up the pieces of my life wouldn't be so easy. Another disaster was about to hit—one of the malicious and vindictive kind, far worse than any abuse my father had ever doled out, and one that would leave me parentless.

SEVEN

....

WELCOME TO...
THE FAMILY FEUD!

The week following my father's memorial service I got two semi-official-looking documents in the mail. Each gave perplexing details on my entitlement to inherit a portion of my father's pension and life insurance, both of which totaled a little more than eighty thousand dollars. But there was no way these documents could have been real. I was pretty sure that I had read somewhere that suicide nullified life insurance. And I knew that my father borrowed against his pension to fix or buy a new car each of the five times he got into an accident, caused by his *retinitis pigmentosa*. These documents had to have been some kind of belated April Fools' prank sent out by a dimwitted practical joker—was it Crazy Eyes?

To make sure I wasn't hallucinating, I called my mother, who told me that the documents were in fact real.

"Your father left me out of it all. This was just his revenge for the divorce," she was quick to point out. "Even in death he found a way to spite me."

"You think that's the whole story? It's not like he left it to PETA or anything," I said, trying to lighten her sour mood.

"He owes me big-time for what he put me through. He treated me like a slave—"

"Yes he did, and you deserve better. How about I share my cut with you? I'm sure Jacob and Erica would do the same. We can split everything equally or something—"

"He knew I have no savings," she said, practically yelling into the phone. "I'll be working till I'm ninety years old!"

(—*Yo, woman, don't be bringing all that noise up in here!*—)

"No you won't. I promise I will take care of all this, but it says I need Dad's death certificate to claim the money. Do you have one?"

"I do. But you have to promise me you won't spend anything yet," she said, her voice colored with shades of desperation and worry. "We need to figure out what we're going to do about this together. I'm worried this'll burn a hole in your brother's pocket."

"It's not really any of my business what he does with it."

"It might be a good idea if I hold on to all the money and distribute it to the three of you as you need it."

"I'm not going to do that just because you're worried about Jacob," I said, alluding to the fact that I was a grown-ass man who didn't need his mommy to handle his financial affairs. I had been doing that on my own since I was fifteen years old, thank you very much.

"I'm just not sure everyone would be so giving once they have the money in their hands," she said rather grimly.

"Of course we would," I said, incredulous she would think such a thing. "We love you very much."

"Well, let's not make any rash decisions. Can you come down this week or next so we can have a family meeting about it?"

"It'll have to be next week, how about Thursday evening? Just send me the death certificate in the meantime so we can at least get the process rolling."

"Okay, I'll do that before the weekend," she said just before we both hung up.

That phone conversation left my head spinning with more questions—not only about my father but my mother as well. Why didn't she trust her own children? I had always had a good relationship with her. And my brother and sister were practically Puritans who'd rather cut off their tongues than tell a lie. Why was she so quick to believe her children's inheritance was all about her and not about us? Was she was angry because her daughter and two sons had DNA that served as a continuous reminder of her dead husband? And why exactly did this man leave us this money? Did he really do it to exact revenge on my mother from beyond the crypt, or did he do it out of love for his children? Or was it a combination of both? My sister was also getting married next year and my brother was in college— both of them with limited funds. Was this inheritance some kind of kamikaze attack on the cost of a wedding planner and student loan payments?

Straight Out of the White Trash Handbook

Monday evening, three days in advance of our big family meeting, I still hadn't received my father's death certificate from my mother and was worried that she might have gotten cold feet and slipped on the way to the mailbox. So, I called her.

"Hey, Mom—just wanted to see if you're alright. I still haven't gotten the death certificate yet. I thought you might be mad at me or something."

"Oh, no, I mailed it out," she said, blatantly ignoring my concern. "But you know, I've been speaking with some advisors and they think that Dad left you that money illegally. He shouldn't have changed you to be his beneficiaries while we were going through our divorce."

"So what does that mean?" I asked while bracing myself for whatever was going to come out of her mouth next.

"It means that you're going to have to wait on that money while I look into what my options are—possibly through the courts."

"Okay, well that might be a problem because there's a hard deadline on this paperwork. We should just file and collect the money. We can hang onto it while you figure out what you're going to do," I said, offering a viable solution that required as little red tape as possible.

"I don't know if everyone is just going to hand over the money once they have it."

"So you *don't* trust us?" I asked, shocked that she was still holding her skeptical stance. I hadn't been dishonest with her since the third grade when I lied about calling my classmate "penis breath."

"I don't know—"

"Well, how much of this money do you actually want, Mom?"

"All of it. I had to put up with that man for thirty years. I deserve it."

(—*Whoa, lady. Ain't nobody deserve that money! Nobody earned it.*—)

"And where do the Rivedal children factor into all of this?" I asked.

"You can do the right thing and sign over your money to me, and I will give all of you help when you need it."

"That doesn't seem like the right thing to do..."

"I need this money more than you. You don't want to see your mother on food stamps," she said, snapping at me.

"You have two jobs and three children who would never allow that to happen," I said, passing up on her invitation to take me on this shameful little guilt trip.

"Don't you take this away from me—"

"I'm not taking anything from you! Shouldn't we just honor his wishes?"

"He wanted to get back at me for leaving him!"

"We don't know that. We don't know what was going on inside his—I don't know, listen, before we all have our meeting, I will look into the legality of Dad leaving us the money—"

"I told you it was illegal!"

"I just want to make sure. And when I get the death certificate, I'm going to file the paperwork, but I promise that when I get the money I will not spend a dime of it, okay?"

"Okay..."

"I'll see you on Thursday."

Was I being an evil son for not giving in to my mother? Or had she turned into a greedy, irrational drama queen? Maybe if we had some accurate legal knowledge we could do the right thing with the money and use this experience to become a stronger family. Over the next few days I got in touch with both my brother and sister over the phone.

"Hey, Erica, did I catch you at a bad time?"

"No, I'm just at work," she replied. She sounded preoccupied helping out customers at her job as a bank teller.

"I assume you got the paperwork from Dad's pension and stuff. Have you talked to Mom about it?" I asked, trying to gauge her feelings about the subject.

"Yeah, I did. She seems to think it's illegal."

"Right. She told me she wanted to take it to court. But I was just thinking we could settle this between the four of us—don't you think?" I asked, still walking on eggshells.

"I was thinking the same thing. I can't just give her all of the money. I have student loans," she said with a hint of frustration in her voice.

"I know. I think we should just split the whole pot four ways—"

"Good idea. Listen, I have to go. I'm working," she said briskly.

"No problem. I will see you at the family meeting."

My brother was a tougher nut to crack. He rarely returned phone calls and only occasionally responded to text messages.

-HEY, JACOB—WAS THINKING WE'D SPLIT OUR MONIES FOUR WAYS WITH MOM. I'LL BRING IT UP AT THE MEETING. YOU COOL WITH THAT?

-SURE.

Due to the diligence and help from my spritely girlfriend, Lara, I studied every piece of New Jersey case law on people who changed the beneficiaries of their estate during divorce proceedings but who died before a ruling could be made. Each case was fascinating and read like the script of a terrible Lifetime made-for-TV movie or an episode of *Jerry Springer*.

In every instance where someone changed their beneficiary from their spouse to their lover, the change was deemed unlawful; but whenever someone changed beneficiaries from their spouse to their children—whether or not they were from that current spouse—the change was upheld in favor of the children.

The evening prior to our big family meeting, I sent my mother all of the research I had in an e-mail in hopes that she would reconsider using the court system to challenge her dead husband's wishes. I didn't want to see her waste thousands of dollars in legal fees to fight a battle that she could never win.

In the wake of losing my father, I didn't have the energy to watch another parent self-destruct. I was optimistic that common sense spelled out in a well thought out e-mail (complete with smiley face emoticons) would help put all this unessential want for judicial interference to rest.

The following day, I made the trip down to New Jersey to have our big family meeting at none other than Cracker Barrel—a little slice of country heaven where rednecks, future diabetics, and my own next-of-kin can settle disputes over chicken fried steak and a plate of biscuits and gravy.

It started off as a pretty typical family lunch. We joked around a little, Jacob gorged himself on mashed potatoes, and I spilled macaroni and cheese all over my pants. It wasn't until dessert that "business" was finally addressed.

"Mom, please don't contest this in court. We can take care of this between ourselves," I said, hoping and praying that the gods of Conventional Wisdom would intercede here on my behalf.

"Joshua, this money belongs to me," she said, taking a very defensive tone and brandishing a dessert fork still carrying pie between its teeth. "And I saw your little e-mail. It only showed cases in your favor!"

(—*Guess you wasn't praying loud enough, dawg...*—)

"That's all there was. I showed you everything!"

"How could you do this to your own mother? After all I've done for you? You don't want to see me out on the street, do you?"

I wished that one of my siblings would speak up, but Erica was terrible at confrontation. And Jacob, who was living with my mother, probably didn't want to risk losing his three hots-and-a-cot. It was up to me to dig in my heels and take one for the team.

"You're not going to be out on the street! You have two jobs, you're getting upwards of eighty thousand dollars from us, you're keeping the house, and you have three children who love you. Enough with the guilt trip stuff. It's not going to work."

"I'm at a loss for words—"

"You and me both," I said, exasperated that this conversation was getting nowhere. "Whatever happened to Dad's death certificate? I never got it."

"I wanted to wait until we had our meeting."

"But you told me you sent it."

"Well, I—"

"So you lied to me?"

(—*Claro, pendejo...*—)

(—No! No. She'll have a good explanation.—)

"I guess I did," she said, lacking any remorse.

"That's it? Well, I still need it," I said, digging my heels even further against this woman I no longer recognized.

"I don't have it. It's at my apartment."

"Well then we need to go get it. I need to file that paperwork today."

"I'm not sure I want to give it to you," she said, her steel blue eyes growing cold, readying herself for an unprecedented showdown with her eldest son.

"I'm sure I can look up Dad's lawyer and get it from him too," I said, defiantly calling her bluff.

"Fine! You want to be like that? Here it is. Take it," she said, irascible in defeat, pulling the death certificate from her purse, throwing it on the table. "Are you happy now?"

No, more like disappointed that the one parent I had always thought of as a pillar of trustworthiness just lied to me twice in one day about money.

Asinine. Fucking. Money. One familial tyrant was on the verge of replacing another. *Viva la revolución.*

Thankfully my sister, who had been playing the role of Switzerland, finally spoke up.

"Mom you're being a little... unreasonable here. Splitting everything four ways without going to court makes the most sense here. Please." She practically begged.

Jacob only spoke up after it was clear how things were shaping up.

"I think that the four-way idea is good. But I'll give you more. You're our mother and you deserve it," he said while dismounting his high horse. That young turk of a strategist had cleverly played his hand with a maneuver straight from the pages of Sun Tzu's *The Art of War.*

"Okay," along with a somber nod in agreement, was the only response my mother could muster up.

The four of us left the Cracker Barrel that day with a promise to one another that we'd put all of this money foolishness behind us and get on with our lives as best we could.

Despite the lying and heated words, I knew that this was totally out of character for my mother. Very soon she would apologize and we would have a stronger relationship than ever before.

The following morning I got a text message from her that read:

-I TALKED 2 MY LAWYER N DECIDED THAT I M GOING 2 MOVE FORWARD N CONTEST THE LIFE INS N PENSION IN COURT. I HOPE U UNDER-STAND.

What exactly was there to understand? This was essentially a lawsuit against her own children who were still mourning the suicide of their father—a conniving move that was straight out of *The White Trash Handbook*.

A Lightning Rod of a Legal Matter

I had always felt a little guilty that I couldn't protect my brother and sister from our father while we were kids. But as an adult I could actually do something for them. I could save them from our mother.

A few days of some serious soul searching came with the realization that if Holly had a lawyer, then I'd have to get one to represent the rest of us. Allowing my mother to lie and steal from us was not an option I could live with.

With help from Lara I secured a meeting in Red Bank, New Jersey, with a lawyer named Annie who practiced family law, which is actually a code name for "battle arena for horribly dysfunctional overgrown children." Ladies and gentlemen, I was now one of those overgrown children.

If I was to succeed in this foray into family law against my mother, I would need the support of both of my siblings.

Erica was my first phone call.

"I have to work that day and I am not going to court against our mother," she said with the firm conviction of a Southern Baptist minister.

"In that case, can you be on the phone for it? She's the one taking us to court. I'm just fighting for Dad's final wishes."

"I don't know," she replied. She sounded obviously conflicted.

"The lawyer does estate law. Dad made you his executrix. What if she could help you with all of that—the paperwork and stuff? Will you be on the phone for that?" I asked.

"I can do that. That sounds fine."

My brother was a different story.

-HEY, MAN. WE NEED TO RESPECT DAD'S WISH-
ES. I'M MEETING WITH A LAWYER. CAN YOU
MAKE IT WHEN I GO?

-I SUPPORT YOUR IDEA. BUT I CAN'T. IT DOESN'T
FEEL RIGHT.

Following that initial meeting with Annie, she
only agreed to take our case provided I understand
she was protecting the final estate of Douglas
Rivedal and wouldn't be engaging in a legal battle
between three children and their mother. Whatever
gets you to sleep at night, lady.

The court date was set for June and even though
I was angry with my mother, I didn't want her to be
left with nothing. I asked Annie to make my mother's lawyer the same offer I had made at the Cracker Barrel. I hoped against hope that by staying true
to my word, she would see that I was trying to do
the right thing and would end this petty feud. But
once more, my Cracker Barrel offer was rejected.

In the months leading up to the court date, I
stopped communicating with my mother completely. I deemed it an affront to my personal dignity to

even entertain having a relationship with someone who so easily lied to me.

In the meantime, her lawyer made frequent Friday afternoon counteroffers to my four-way split proposal that included a larger share of proceeds in my mother's favor. Her demands included: a) That her children share in her expense for post-suicide mortgage payments on the house she and my father owned together. b) That her children share in the cost of an unpaid public service bill in my father's name. c) That her children share my father's funeral expenses. d) That her children defray some of the cost of my brother's college education.

Some of these requests were reasonable, but I couldn't figure out why my mother needed a lawyer to make them. We were capable of solving this kind of stuff on our own.

Hurt and feeling slighted, I responded to each of these counteroffers with a "no." There was a slim chance my siblings and I could be left with nothing if the court ruled in my mother's favor. But I wanted what I thought was fair or nothing at all.

I wish I could say that the dissolution of our mother-son bond didn't come with a cost; but my heart, still on the mend, couldn't take the trauma of being ripped out once again by anyone else. I found myself losing trust in relationships with some of my friends and even with my girlfriend, who could see I was struggling.

"Josh, you know I love you, but if you need to take a break from us right now to deal with your family stuff, I understand. I will always be here for you," she said casually as we walked home one night after dinner at a little Italian restaurant in our neighborhood.

(—*Listen, homie, once you let her go she ain't coming back.*—)
(—I know but she's all I've got.—)
(—*You have us, papi.*—)
(—I don't know what I want... I'm scared.—)
(—*Confess with your mouth and you will be saved.*—)

"No. I'm fine. I can do this. And I want to be with you. Forever. Please don't bring it up again." The absoluteness of those words was belied by the queasiness in my stomach and the thick irresolution encumbering my voice as I spoke. The blue in her eyes had flecks of cynicism. She wasn't convinced I was telling the truth. So I scooped her into my arms, stared deeply into her eyes, and kissed her soft lips with every ounce of passion that lived inside my body. She was still my girlfriend, my friend, my ally...for now.

EIGHT

····································

RIVEDAL V. RIVEDAL

Picture, if you can, a lovely summer morning in Toms River, New Jersey: hummingbirds singing a bright melody in exquisite harmony; squirrels chattering away while dining over a princely meal of berries, acorns, and pine cones; and the sun shining ever so slightly through a voluminous cluster of puffy white clouds. Truly, one could not ask for a more beautiful day to go air their private grievances with their mother in public at the county courthouse.

In a long hallway outside of our designated courtroom, and while waiting for the festivities to begin, I saw my mother, out of the corner of my eye, making a beeline toward me. Her arms were at full cock for an embrace. The thought of offering such affection to Ms. Benedict Arnold made me sick to my stomach, so I ducked into the women's handicapped bathroom where I could wait and dry heave until our case was called.

(—*You shall honor thy mother...*—)
(—Put a lid on it, Churchy. Not today.—)

Before being ushered into the courtroom by Annie, I got my first glimpse of Holly's attorney—a thirty-something petite woman not terribly unattractive, yet with the stone-cold gaze of a serial killer and the jowls of a small pit bull. On the right-hand side of the dimly lit courtroom sat my mother, my brother, and Pit Bull, while I sat with Annie and my sister on the left. Each of us was dressed in our Sunday best, ready for our Revelational Day of Judgment in the grandest of style.

We listened to the tail end of the preceding trial, a boorish tale of unpaid child support, a marriage annulment, and the question of child paternity that would make even my old friend, Maury Povich, shudder in disgust. Just as the judge was about to drop his gavel to make his ruling official, Pit Bull pulled Annie aside and asked if they could speak alone outside the courtroom. Within seconds Annie returned.

"Your mother and her lawyer want to negotiate a settlement. Is that okay with you two?" Annie asked ever so calmly in a smooth sotto voce.

Erica and I looked at each other, both of us equally astonished. "What about the judge?" I asked Annie.

"No judges. Just us," she answered.

Both sides had been driving at each other full speed in a three-month battle of chicken, and Pit Bull was the one who finally swerved. She must have known her client was going to lose and now was the time to negotiate for her thirty pieces of silver.

The two lawyers ushered us into a private room where we all sat around a long rectangular conference table. The prologue to our negotiations was sung in sparse and dissonant six-part harmony, with Pit Bull on the descant—lyrics being the customary "Hellos" and "How-do-you-dos" with a "My, this weather is nice" for good measure. Somehow Pit Bull pushed her way to the front of the stage flashing a new engagement ring, singing a piercing and interminable solo about her impending nuptials and the diamond-encrusted hood ornament weighing down her left hand.

The afternoon consisted of onerous and lengthy deliberation over a fair split of my father's meager assets and every petty detail was brought into play—his dinged-up old car, his vacation pay, and legal fees incurred by *both* my mother and father. We reached a preliminary agreement that the four of us would share evenly in the costs of my father's remaining debt along with the aggregate of my parents' legal fees.

(—*Is she gonna ask y'all to split the contents of his underwear drawer too?*—)
(—*Esto es mierda. Complete shit.*—)

To the matter of the life insurance and pension, Pit Bull *demanded* her client receive half of the proceeds while allowing her client's children to split the remainder however they saw fit, provided that we took over our father's fifty percent stake in the house.

I didn't need to attend Fancy Boston Upstairs Lawyer College to know that Pit Bull was furtively showing herself to be a master negotiator. Her offer was designed to look like a candy-coated act of kindness, an "opportunity" for three poor, fatherless children to acquire equity in a house. But in reality, her tactic was cold-blooded, a chance to alleviate her client's financial burden on a house that she couldn't afford to live in while forcing us to swallow the bitter pill of another expense.

"*That's* not going to work. No freaking way. We're going split the life insurance and pension four ways and you can keep your split of the house," I shouted, my anger spilling over onto the conference table and all over Pit Bull's best-laid plans. Annie reined me in without matching my tone and respectfully rephrased my adamant request in a friendlier manner, acquiescing on Pit Bull's request that we take ownership in the house.

Holly and her guard dog happily accepted Annie's counteroffer. We had essentially negotiated 360 degrees, back to my original offer with nothing gained. Thousands of dollars were lost, along with any semblance of respect I had for my mother.

As we were leaving the conference room, the Judas anxiously waited by the door so we could talk, as if a legal settlement could erase the last three months. But I hurried past her and found myself again in the women's handicapped bathroom.

How did I get to such a dismal place in my life so quickly? Coming out of high school and high on optimism, I thought by the time I turned twenty-five I would have it all together. After a couple of years singing on Broadway, I would have scored a few bit parts on *Law & Order*, and transitioned seamlessly from having my own television show, *Jake & the Fat Man: 2.0*, to being cast with Will Smith in the summer's biggest blockbuster. After which, my getaway home in the Hamptons would be featured in *Better Homes & Gardens*, and my face would grace the cover of the *National Enquirer* as Bigfoot's not-so-secret lover. Not to mention, I'd have my perfect wife and perfect family by my side to share in my success.

But instead, I somehow only managed to perform in an assortment of minor league theatre and on one embarrassing reality television show, then got sidetracked by my father's suicide and a court date with my mother that had me locked inside of a women's bathroom hovered over the toilet spewing vomit laced with tears.

The conclusion to my journey into the ring of family law was bittersweet. On one hand, I was an orphan with no parents and no place to call home, but on the other hand I was a prizefighter who had defeated a formidable opponent on a technical knockout at the end of fifteen rounds. Though my ribs were fractured and my eyes bruised and bloody, I went the distance and was still standing.

I spent my victory party back at my New York apartment, huddled around my sixty-thousand-dollar check, along with the shambles my life had become, wondering if that six and those four zeros could help put me back together.

NINE

....

THE PARABLE OF THE TALENTS: THE HIT BROADWAY MUSICAL!

Every so often during my daily fantasy about winning the lottery, I wonder if the people who've actually won big money are significantly happier after hitting their lucky payday. Each of the major television networks has done their own version of "The Lotto: A Special Interest Story" about some interchangeable idiot named Billy Rae Jinkins who won hundreds of millions of dollars playing the Powerball only to go bankrupt in ten months after blowing all of his winnings on lavish trips to Burger King, his needy neighbors, his brother's girlfriend's uncle's autistic cousin, ten Porsches, a gold-plated Hello Kitty toilet, and an

Olympic-sized swimming pool in the shape of Telly Savalas' head.

Billy Rae, now destitute, ends up selling his only granddaughter into slavery so he can keep up with his diabetes medication. Subsequently, he opens a meth lab with the very last of his cash only to get busted by the Feds and then thrown in jail. In his exclusive prison interview with Diane Sawyer in prime time, Billy Rae stifles back tears and with great conviction says, "I've never been more miserable. Dagnabbit, I wish I'd never bought that winning lotto ticket!"

In the days and weeks following the settlement of my father's estate, I was feeling a little like Billy Rae after winning my own $60,000 Powerball (minus the Hello Kitty toilet, of course). After dividing up my father's things, including his money, I thought his death and the direction of my life might actually start to make a little sense. But having this money was like a dark cloud of uncertainty hanging over my head. Was I supposed to spend this money or get rid of it? This financial endowment was the only remotely positive memory I had of him that didn't involve his lack of social graces or one his many famous pratfalls due to his partial blindness.

This money was the nicest gift my father had ever given me outside of not aborting me, feeding me, and occasionally throwing a football around with my younger self. He could have left everything to the church or some right-wing militant Christian organization, but instead he chose to give me something that didn't come with a card signed by my mother, who had carelessly forged his signature.

This conundrum of what to do with my money had me leafing through my Bible for the first time in over a decade. I was reminded of the biblical Parable of the Talents as told by Jesus (the Jewish carpenter of yore, not the Dominican baseball player).

To make the Parable of the Talents a bit more relatable to our Muslim, Atheist, and non-Bible reading friends, I will tell it reimagined as a 1980's blockbuster Broadway musical starring the supremely talented Colm Wilkinson.

A wealthy hedge fund manager, also a Scottish lord by the name Lawrence Wankersford III (played by Wilkinson), was leaving his four-story Brownstone apartment on the Upper East Side of Manhattan to do business in Monte Carlo for a year. Just before he departed, he loaned three of his most loyal yet peculiar servants "talents," which in the 1980s was an interchangeable term for a large sum of money.

To the first servant (played by Mandy Patinkin), a handsome, failed former Argentine revolutionary, he gave five talents. To the second servant (played by Michael Crawford), a horribly disfigured and eccentric brute with a heart of gold and a knack for songwriting, he gave two talents. And to the third servant (played by Angela Lansbury), a baker and lusty gal with an insatiable appetite for flesh, he gave one talent.

When his year in Monte Carlo was over, Lawrence came back to Manhattan with a fresh tan from the French Riviera sun and majority ownership of a Monaco football team. Much to his delight, he found that the first two servants invested their talents in IBM, Berkshire Hathaway, and a series of high performing junk bonds that made their talents grow exponentially.

Lawrence was so pleased with the first two servants that he bestowed upon them honorary titles of Gentlemen within his house, more talents to invest, and a vacation in Martha's Vineyard.

But the third servant put her one and only talent under a mattress in the basement of his

Brownstone apartment. Risk and trust in the American stock market were not in her DNA—she simply wanted to return his money to him, assuming that doing so would please him. But Lawrence grew furious with her for being all too cautious and punished her by taking away her talent. Furthermore, he expelled her from his service, forcing her to live out her days as a poor purveyor of mysterious and delectable meat pies.

The moral of the original story Jesus was telling may very well have been "use it or lose it." And he may have been making a valid point.

TEN

....

A VISIT FROM AN OLD
FRENEMY

To make my fiscal dilemma even worse, the night following my court settlement with Holly, while fast asleep I had an eerie dream about my father that seemed all too real. He appeared as a blond-haired Adonis-like Viking with sparkling white teeth, long flowing hair, and a set of well-toned abs on which you could wash your dirty laundry. Despite his strange yet pleasing appearance, there was something intangible about him, almost spiritual, that made me believe this figure to be my father. I had met this golden butterfly when he was only an ill-tempered little caterpillar. We stood face to face in the middle of a graveyard littered with unmarked tombstones. He held out a giant wad of folded cash that I could not quite reach. His lips formed words without sound, the shape of which I couldn't quite understand.

That night I woke in a cold sweat and gasping for air. I found some much-needed relief at the sight of the green digital numbers on the alarm clock beside my bed. It was just a dream. Thank God. However, that feeling of respite was temporary and only to be found during daylight hours. For the next two weeks, I awoke every night from that same dream, clammy and terrified at what was happening inside my head. I could only conclude that either my father wanted to scare me by invading my dreams, or he was trying to give me some kind of a sign to tell me what to do with his money.

In early July, these unwelcome dreams and financial worries were coming to a head. One night, I woke at 4 a.m. following another dream about my dead father, shivering and praying to a God I wasn't sure I believed in, "Please make this 'Ghost Dad' stop tormenting me." While wrapping up the ostensible one-sided conversation, my thoughts were consumed with the outcome of everything that had transpired with my father. With heavy eyelids and a heart equally so, I was reminded, quite unexpectedly so, of the promise I made to myself just after his death: Live. Chase your dreams even harder. Make your life count.

My vow had fallen by the wayside, forgotten due to the all-encompassing legal proceedings of the last few months.

CHANGES

That same morning at 8 a.m., I was still ruminating over the state of my life. It had become a futile survival of living paycheck to paycheck as a faceless zombie who served salmon burgers to the wealthy Upper East Side elite while my creative life sat in a three-year slumber, possibly never to awaken, while heated arguments with my girlfriend over peccadillos became a regular occurrence that led me from neglect to avoiding her altogether. This meager existence had me questioning whether emerging from the shadow of my father's suicide and living life was even worth the trouble. I was lacking inspiration for any sort of meaningful change in my life, and it seemed as if there were few opportunities in society for an uneducated struggling actor with a messy personal life. Peeling away layers of goose down and cotton, I arose like a machine on autopilot to begin going through the motions of my usual daily routine. I started off with a hot shower while music from my iTunes library played on full blast. Stepping out of the tub, and while massaging my scalp vigorously with a towel in front of the mirror, *Changes* by rapper Tupac Shakur began to play.

A STARK NAKED REVELATION

Wiping down my birthday suit and staring at the reflection in front of me, the treble of the piano in the song brought out to play the little voices living in my head, which had grown more crotchety and insistent since the settlement with my mother.

(—I'm tired of struggling, being sad, having nothing.—)

(—*Naked you came from your mother's womb, naked you will depart.*—)

(—No. I have to do something to change things up. The money.—)

(—*Don't even think about it, dawg. It's blood money.*—)

(—*Oy ye, estúpido. You're just going to find a way to screw it up.*—)

(—Maybe I won't. Maybe it isn't blood money if I use it well.—)

To do what? To honor his memory? To invest in myself? To find some of that inspiration I was looking for? With the inheritance from my father I could buy those opportunities.

Electrified and reinvigorated by this little light bulb moment, I kicked open my bathroom door and sprinted buck naked down the little hallway in my shoe-box-sized apartment in search of something with which to write. Time was of the essence. I needed to jot down all the new thoughts swirling around in my head before the light bulb flickered out. With a red Crayola crayon and a mini sketchpad in hand, I scribbled little bullet points of only the essentials:

- A college education (so I can get out of the restaurant business)
- A retirement portfolio (so I'll never be old and on food stamps)
- A new computer (need to replace the outdated turd I'm currently using)
- New head-shots (current pictures make me look like a prepubescent girl)
- Writing class (can fulfill secret wish to pursue professionally, yikes)

- A solo getaway (escape familiar surroundings and find some life/career inspiration)

With a few strokes of a crayon, I began to feel like a man on a mission toward something huge and unprecedented—like maybe a movement that would change the world or a revelation on the meaning of life. Since every historically significant event generally required clothing, I found myself rummaging through the top drawer of my dresser looking for some of my own to wear.

Searching for a pair of boxer briefs beneath a smattering of unmated socks, a wall of nostalgia washed over me like an ocean wave—reminding me that the bottom drawer was full of my father's personal effects that I took from his bedroom the day after he died. I hadn't looked at or even thought about them since the day I brought them into my apartment. Sliding open that bottom drawer, I carefully removed a few old *Life* magazines with covers featuring Diana Ross, Henry Kissinger, the inventor of the Polaroid camera, and Nikita Khrushchev. I also took out a copy of one of his old driver's licenses and an enormous, dusty American flag that the U.S. Government gave my father in honor of

Haakon's burial in Arlington National Cemetery. The last of what I pulled out were three old photo albums that I, until this day, had never viewed.

Inside the first photo album were pictures of my father from the early 1970s while on vacation with some of his friends and family, a few years before he met my mother. He had an odd, thin mustache and looked much happier than I had ever seen him. While thumbing my way to the back of the album, a thin leather-bound booklet that I didn't recognize slid out from between the pages of the plastic sleeves. It was light brown and threadbare. The pages were yellow and tattered, and the whole of it was held together by a rubber band. Inside the cover was my father's trademark handwriting—neat little words in all capital letters.

This was his old diary. In it were the childhood games he used to play, the names of some of his old neighborhood friends, and the girls with whom he was smitten during his Lutheran elementary school days:

MY FIRST CIGARETTE WAS GREAT. BUT SINCE I'M THIRTEEN, I WAS SCARED TO SMOKE WHEN MY PARENTS GOT HOME SO I THREW IT INSIDE OUR PIANO. MY DAD SMELLED IT AND GOT IT OUT IN TIME. I

DIDN'T EVEN GET IN TROUBLE. THEY JUST TOLD ME
NOT TO BURN THE HOUSE DOWN. NEAT!

As I flipped through the pages, his writing became more perfunctory and his dated entries were few and far between. Toward the back he wrote about his early twenties and talked briefly about his time at Park College in Kansas City, Missouri.

He listed all of the jobs he had ever held (teacher, substitute teacher, amateur lawn care specialist, store clerk), but what he seemed most enthusiastic about was the law. He wanted to be a lawyer. A few pages were marked only with the words, "I WANT MORE OUT OF LIFE," written over and over again—reminiscent of Jack Nicholson's deranged character in *The Shining*.

My father almost married a long-term girlfriend, a woman who was in love with him whom he found "UTTERLY BEAUTIFUL BUT EMOTIONALLY UNSTABLE." He also doubted whether he could commit to just one woman, and subsequently broke up with his long-term girlfriend at a coffee shop to keep her from going on a "PSYCHOTIC RAMPAGE." On the last page was a list of places he had traveled to: Germany, England, and Italy; along with a short list of places he needed to visit before he died: Jerusalem, Norway, and Vancouver.

I learned more about my father reading twenty pages of his diary than I ever had in the twenty-five years I had known him. Conversations about television shows, family members, or his opinions on biblical doctrine always came easy, but we never talked about anything deeper. Who he truly was, how he felt about women, or what he wanted out of life—those were things that only a skilled and meticulous excavator could uncover. And my father didn't keep company with any of those scholarly diggers.

(—*The rotten apple don't fall too far from the tree, my dude.*—)

(—Oh, god, do not say that.—)

This was the first time I had ever met my father, a flawed man, but a human being with hopes and dreams. My chest pounded with sharp pangs of pity, my heart ached for this man. This diary was damning evidence, beyond a reasonable doubt, that he had given up on himself a long time ago. He never made a real effort to become a lawyer or anything else for that matter. And he never made it to Jerusalem, Norway, or Vancouver.

What happened to the man in the diary? He grew up, took a dead-end job with the State of New Jersey, married Holly, found religion, had three kids, and killed himself. What turned him into the angry shell of a person who taunted me as a child and who now haunted me as an adult?

I carefully put away all of my father's personal effects then lay down on my couch. With my hands behind my head, and my eyes closed, I tried to picture what my own life would look like in thirty-five years. Due to my lack of sleep the previous night, I was fast asleep within minutes and toe-to-toe with Ghost Dad once again.

ELEVEN

....

NEW WATERS

This particular dream started out the same as all the others. But this time he wasn't holding a wad of cash, but a leather-bound diary as if he was preparing to read aloud from its pages. He appeared to be in a foul mood, his face red and covered in sweat like a fire-and-brimstone preacher of old. Before he could say a word, I leapt from the graveyard and literally flew toward a place to which I knew, instinctively, neither of us had ever been. That phantom menace, my dead father, followed me till I touched down in what looked like a rainforest. A massive gorge with a river sprawled out at its bottom separated the luxuriant Technicolor paradise from an endless and ashen, barren field.

Ghost Dad, dejected and desperate, stood on the other side of the gorge, unable to cross over to meet

me. Overcome with sympathy for this pitiful apparition, I began searching for ways to help him cross.
Just as I turned my back on my father to venture
into the rainforest to find some help, a soft wind
snuck up from behind and whispered in my ear.

"You cannot help him enter until you learn the
secrets of the rainforest," said the wind, tickling the
fine little hairs on my earlobe. I spun around as fast
as I could in order to catch a glimpse of whomever
was speaking, but the wind grew violent and
knocked me to the ground, causing me to wake
from my sleep.

Ensuing days were spent ridden with apprehen-
sion, while working to decipher the meaning of
that dream so different from all the others. For the
sake of a good night's sleep and my personal sanity,
these appearances had to stop. I had to uncover the
"secrets" of the rainforest before he returned.

TWELVE

··

DIARY OF A CRAZY
WHITE DUDE
(AND OTHER RAMBLINGS)

Right or wrong, I interpreted the "Secrets of the Rainforest" dream to mean that I should get the hell out of New York City and go somewhere my father had never been. (There was no way his ghost could haunt me if his body hadn't been there too, right?) The only places I knew for certain that he had never been were Jerusalem, Norway, and Vancouver.

Earlier in the month I had made plans with Lara to take a short trip to Portland, Oregon, in late July. For her, it was a chance to visit some family she hadn't seen in a while, but for me it was an opportunity to escape the familiar surroundings and the madness of the past three months. I needed—no required some fresh air. Vancouver in British Columbia, only a few hundred miles from Portland by car, would now be a part of my trip's itinerary.

My plan was to fly into Portland five days ahead of Lara and take a solo road trip up through Washington State and into Vancouver, allowing enough time for self-reflection and a little sightseeing. This road trip would also prove to be an adequate test of my self-reliance, in case Lara or anyone else I loved self-destructed or walked out of my life again. The perfect way to tap into my inner Henry David Thoreau, with the Pacific Northwest serving as my Walden Pond.

THE OPEN ROAD

In a matter of weeks I found myself at John F. Kennedy International Airport, quite pleased with myself. I followed through with my plans and was traveling solo for the very first time just like a big boy. In a few days I'd be in an entirely different country, and would presumably be rid of Ghost Dad forever.

As I was boarding the plane, I got an infuriating text message from my mother:

- I LOVE YOU AND I'M PRAYING FOR YOU.

She couldn't be serious. What did she want me to say? That everything was all better and we could go back to being a family? Not until I got my apology. I was determined to win this passive aggressive standoff.

(—*Love those who betray you...*—)
(—Except I'm on vacation right now. That shit can wait.—)

When finally in Portland, and as irony would have it, the rental car company gave me the exact same color, make, and model of Toyota Yaris that my father owned until he died.

My hotel was near the airport and I would've reached it sooner had I not missed the highway off-ramp. I spent a full hour making nothing but right turns until I took a left that got me on the right track. By the time I checked in and put my bags down, I was completely exhausted. Plans to explore the bar scene in Portland turned into having a burger at the Red Robin across the street from the hotel followed by a savory dessert of two menthol cigarettes in the parking lot. That night in my room I began a travel diary, which I befittingly named *Diary of a Crazy White Dude.*

Day One:

All in all I saw some cool mountains out of my plane window today, which caused me to realize that I am agnostic. It's been a long time coming. I don't know about Jesus or God or the Bible in the same exact way as I was raised (I'm open to it), but I do believe the world was created at some point—by whom or for what purpose I don't know. Maybe we'll never know, but we should keep working toward finding out.

Science may be a key into understanding the "how," but we may never know the "why." There seem to be some profound mysteries at the root of a lot of scientific theory, but we've made many breakthroughs in the past few hundred years and are progressing pretty fast. I hope we can continue to do so and as individuals have a spiritual enlightenment and understanding of why we're here. Can we blend the spiritual and science? There's gotta be some kind of bridge between the two...

On the connecting flight to Portland, I sat beside a young couple who were getting ready to have their first child. It made me think about having one... and I'm freaking great with kids, but I gotta wonder if the family unit is something imposed on us as a culture. Or is it natural and an inevitable yearning of life?

Just a few thoughts (answers would be nice) but some good ones for the day. But time to stop and put my head to the pillow. Peace and love.

The next morning I hit the road early with my travel partner, the companionable companion, Solitude. It took longer to cross into Washington State, but only because I made another wrong turn that took me two hours out of my way. I scrapped my plans to drive up through the coastal hamlets. Instead, I took a detour directly toward Mount Rainer National Park and arrived an hour before sundown. Later that night in Bellevue, Washington, after a very full day, I wrote my second diary entry:

Day Two:
After making it out of Portland, I stopped at a little diner called Mintzy's or Poopsies. I can't remember, but I may have taken a picture. The food was fine. I had a mediocre French dip sandwich and some good coffee. I saw a lot of old country folk at this place and thought, "God, I hope that's not me in forty years." The freaking guy who is taking a trip alone and who barely has any friends doesn't want to be like someone

else. How odd. Get some friends, asshole. Learn to be more social or less awkward or do a better job of faking it. To me it would be sad to be in my sixties and living in Washington in the sparse areas and hoping for good deals at Wal-Mart. I need to start making my fortune now so I don't end up like that. I also need to live in the moment and enjoy the day. A nice balance would be good. Planning for the future seems like what I do often and am down on myself or pass through the moment without thinking...

Walking through a bunch of trails at Rainer, I can only imagine all the animals and Native Americans that passed through this area for centuries before Whitey got there. These people lived off the land and worshipped their ancestors and knew each other, their culture, and the day they were in. I aspire to that kind of familiarity. While trying to leave the park, I took a series of wrong turns (AGAIN) which led me to the Silver Falls, a glacier waterfall. I felt like I was in a scene from the Shire of Middle-earth. There was no yesterday or tomorrow, no Ghost Dad, no suicide, or Pit Bull; only the river flowing over the falls and splashing onto the rocks below.

Alright, man, I'm beat. That's probably enough for tonight. Peace, dude.

The following morning I wandered around Seattle's famed Pike Place market and drank my body weight in coffee and espresso at some of the mom-and-pop cafes in the area. The best part of the day was a drive northeast of Seattle through some wine country. Wiped out from copious amounts of wine and coffee consumption, I spent my evening sequestered in my Bellevue hotel.

Day Three:

On to Seattle and the Space Needle. Pretty cool and definitely a beautiful city. The Needle was alright, but I only stayed for maybe twenty minutes on the observation deck. It's like why am I up here to see a bunch of four-story buildings...

I loved going to the wineries, but it's mad weird going to a place like that by yourself. No one knows how to look at you and everyone's like why is this guy here by himself? What a loser. Let's see you people try to do something completely on your own...

One of the wineries, La Grand Reve, was basically a storefront that had a very knowledgeable winemaker giving a tasting to a family of older parents, maybe in their early sixties, and their daughter in her mid-thirties. They were nice, but the dad bothered the hell out of me. He seemed like this hardcore uptight guy who knew everything about everything and had to tell you about it. The wife was nice and tried to include me, a loner, into their laughter and jokes. I felt bad for the daughter because she looked like the dad with thinning hair and pockmarked skin. You knew she was single. Not trying to be mean, just telling it like it is.

I know I'm a little judgmental, but I'm working through it. It's my Baptist roots. Speaking of which, no thoughts of family today until now, but no more clarity on life stuff either. Hmm. Either way I think I can go to bed happy with the day that I had. And that's enough for the day. Peace, homes.

That night, Ghost Dad once again came to visit me in my sleep.

THIRTEEN

....

COUGHING UP UNFINISHED BUSINESS

We stood on opposite sides of a ravine that had a mighty river flowing through its base. On my side was a lush rainforest painted with waterfalls and a thick, green canopy. On Ghost Dad's side was a desolate field colored in hues of brown and gray. We did absolutely nothing but stand perfectly still, each of us waiting for the other to do or say something. Finally, Ghost Dad placed his right hand behind his head, then brought it down in front of his chest. Floating just above his outstretched palm like skywriting were the words "TELL MY STORY" in large black capital letters. As I opened my mouth to ask the apparition the meaning of this message, a violent cough came over me, which caused me to wake from my sleep.

JOSH RIVEDAL

FOURTEEN

....

WELCOME TO CANADA, EH?

I figured that either I was going crazy or Ghost Dad had followed me clear across the country. But I wasn't going to wait any longer to find out. I scrapped my plans to stay in the Seattle area for a second day and was back on the road by 8 a.m. the next morning, destined for Vancouver. I arrived at the Canadian border a little before noon. The lines of cars waiting to exit the United States weren't terribly long. My lane featured an overzealous border services officer, Officer Aaron, who may have gotten his training from one of the *Police Academy* movies.

"Do you have alcohol, firearms, or tobacco?" he barked as I pulled up to his booth.

"No, Officer A, eh? I left all that stuff back at the compound," I said with a smile.

His face turned the color of a maple leaf. "Excuse me?" he asked.

"I was just being silly."

"You were just being silly, what?"

"I was just being silly... sir?"

"That's more like it." He began to thoroughly inspect around and under my vehicle. "Did you drive all the way from California?"

"No, I just rented this in Portland, Oregon... sir."

"What's your purpose of the visit and where are you staying?"

"My father just died and I'm taking a little trip to Vancouver to honor his memory." I had to make full use of the sympathy card in my back pocket.

"How did he die?"

"Terminal gonorrhea," I said with a straight face. It was unthinkable that this guy had the audacity to ask me such a personal question.

His face turned to horror. "Seriously?" he asked, looking down at his crotch and then back up at me.

"No. It was suicide."

"Wow," he said, squirming in discomfort at hearing the "S" word. "You're not going to do that up here, are you?"

"Only if I have to keep talking to you."

"Alright, get out of here, eh."

Douche. Bag.

After crossing the border, I drove a short spell through farm country and over a few large rivers until I found my way into downtown Vancouver, a beautiful and culturally diverse city that felt quaint and friendly despite its multipurpose high-rises, skyscrapers, and its half a million people. I explored as much of the city as I could and at the end of a late dinner, I went for a long walk at the edge of the waterfront. The moon was peering from behind some clouds, shining off of the seaplanes and oil tankers that were resting up for the night. The grunts and groans of two junkies fornicating on a sidewalk off in the distance made for a sweet melody that capped off the end of a magical night.

Back at my hotel and completely drained from a full day of walking, sightseeing, and a live junkie porn show, I promptly fell asleep, fully dressed in my travel clothes. While I slept, the brawny Specter of Scandinavia, my dead father, appeared to me yet again.

FIFTEEN

....

NO ESCAPE

O nce again, we were on opposite sides of the ravine. This time we were both seated cross-legged facing one another and he was crying. His tears flowed down into the gorge, causing the river to rise to the level at which we were sitting. As the water touched my toes, he placed his right hand in front of his chest and the words "TELL MY STORY" in black capital letters appeared above his outstretched palm again. But before I could question him, a strong gust of wind blew into my nostrils, causing me to choke and wake from my slumber.

SIXTEEN

A WALK THROUGH THE (JAPANESE) GARDEN OF EDEN

I looked over at the alarm clock and it was 7 a.m. and time to get ready for my last day in the Vancouver area.

(—*You traveled three thousand miles and your pops is still hanging around?*—)
(—There's got to be a reason he's here.—)
(—*There is a reason. Eres estúpido, a dumbass...*—)

After a quick shower and a light breakfast of little sausages and cheese, I headed out to the Nitobe Memorial Garden, a traditional Japanese Tea and Stroll garden located on the edge of the University of British Columbia's campus. It described itself as "a place of reflection, where each step reveals a new harmony, the garden is designed to suggest a span of time—a day, a week, or a lifetime—with a beginning, choice of paths, and ending."

A revelation of new harmony was exactly what I needed. I went to the Pacific Northwest to live deliberately and to front only the essential facts of life. But so far my trip had been little more than self-indulgent. I had no more clarity about my life or its purpose and I was losing an increasing amount of sleep due to my father's incessant enigmatic appearances, which I still couldn't decipher.

Arriving on campus, I inched along a few winding roads that led me to a secluded little back corner of the school's grounds. It was here that walls of a garden were erect, separating the undisturbed serenity within its core from the chaos of the rest of the world. A small stone path led to a large and stoic wooden gate that warmly invited me to pass through its threshold and into what looked like the Japanese Garden of Eden.

One large circular footpath, lined with neatly pruned cherry trees and red cedars, enclosed a number of smaller paths and bridges made of logs and planks that crossed over a pond at the center of the garden. At several junctions along the inner footpaths were old stone lanterns sprinkled throughout. A solitary wooden pavilion sat near the garden's center. At any moment I expected to see a Japanese Adam and Eve emerge from the brush wearing nothing but maple leaves.

I wandered aimlessly through the garden absorbing the peacefulness of everything through my fingers: the hairy moss on the ground, the small waterfalls making perfect little ripples into the water, large rocks resting along the lake, and the exterior of a dignified and ancient-looking teahouse. The tranquil energy flowing through me, given from the rocks and trees, brought something inside me to life—something almost supernatural. This force felt almost prescient and told me that inside this garden was the answer to the many lingering questions beleaguering my fragile mind.

With urgency, I circled around the outer edge of the garden, in the heated pursuit of anything—a clue, a hint, an insight—but with no such luck. I circled around a second time and still nothing. The vigor of my inner spark began to ferment into heavy fatigue and I paused my search.

I approached a seven-story Pagoda, a solitary and tired piece of stone that looked as if he needed a friend to sit at its feet and keep him company for a bit. I sat cross-legged at his base facing the pond, resting my head against his chiseled torso. Within moments, my eyelids became heavy and fought to resist gravity's pull but finally succumbed to the laws of physics. I fell into a deep sleep and there I was welcomed by the Adonis Viking, Ghost Dad.

SEVENTEEN

....

A CLUE

We stood on opposite sides of the same ravine as we had in previous encounters. He was crying yet again, but was enraged like the man I knew from my childhood. His tears flowed down into the gorge and caused the river to rise above my ankles.

"Why are you doing this to me?" I asked. I could finally speak to this infamous and unwelcome specter. He wouldn't answer and the water rose to my knees. "You're ruining my life. Leave me alone!" He didn't respond, and the river rose to my waist. "What do you want? What do you want from me!?" And with outstretched arms and open palms side by side he conjured up more skywriting in black capital letters. Above his right hand was the word

"TELL" and above his left hand were the words "MY STORY."

"What are you talking about? I can't. I wouldn't know how."

"Then write it down," he said as the river rose to my chest.

"How am I supposed to do that? I don't understand what you want," I answered. I was now in tears myself.

"Figure it out. Tell the world." And with that he floated away until he melted into the sun. The river had now risen past the level of my head and engulfed my entire body. I awoke sweating and lying face up on the ground.

EIGHTEEN

....

A HOSTAGE CRISIS

Pulling myself up to a sitting position, I braced myself for support against my new friend, the seven-story stone Pagoda. Was this the clue I was looking for? Was this really my father or a figment of my imagination? Wiping the sweat from my brow, I wondered what he could possibly want me to say about him. Everything I knew about him involved yelling, religion, disappointment, and suicide—not exactly a compelling tale or strong legacy to leave behind.

A trip to Vancouver did not rid me of Ghost Dad but showed me that he would continue to hold my dreams hostage until I did exactly what he wanted. There would be *no* negotiating with my nighttime terrorist.

NINETEEN

···

THE ORPHAN'S REVOLT

On a flight from Portland back to New York City, I racked my sleep-deprived brain contemplating all the ways I could write and tell the story of my dead father.

(—*You could do a rhyme over a sample of "Stuntin' Like My Daddy."*—)

(—I don't know... he wasn't a big rap fan...—)

(—*How 'bout an essay, ese?*—)

(—That sounds about as interesting as an ingrown toenail. Next!—)

(—*Make him proud and deliver a sermon.*—)

(—The Reverend Josh Rivedal. Good one. You officially suck.—)

In the weeks leading up to my Vancouver trip, I had been considering using some of my father's money to sign up for a playwriting class. Maybe I could write some sort of biographical play about him and cast myself in it, effectively killing two birds with one stone: unemployment and a dead nuisance. I love it when a plan comes together.

THE PRESSURE TO PERFORM

While the nature of my ongoing nightmarish reveries with my dead father was becoming clearer, the rest of the relationships in my life dissolved into something of a murky mess.

The only conversations I was having with my sister were about the prompt distribution of my father's assets. Phone calls to my brother went unanswered and text messages like, HEY, MAN I MISS YOU, CALL ME, and HEY, DUDE, LOVE YOU. LET'S TALK SOON went unreturned. Despite weekly text messages from my mother, I vowed that I would not communicate with her until after the house sold and all its proceeds were split as per the letter of our settlement back in June. I would wait as long as it took. Anything I'd have to say to her would be accompanied with a heavy dose of venom, and the last thing I needed was another potential lawsuit on my hands.

My five-year anniversary with Lara was also fast approaching and I was feeling an increasing amount of pressure to ask her to marry me. When we first moved in together, I was a struggling actor of limited means and promised to propose once I had enough money for a ring. Now that I had a little extra cash in my pocket, courtesy of my dead father, there was no more financial excuse. Lara's impatience with me grew to a head on the eve of our anniversary.

"I'd like to reopen the conversation about marriage... *us* getting married," Lara stated. Her eyes were unsmiling and pensive. Her voice was tempered with a subtle misgiving, perhaps sensing that this was not something I was ready to talk about.

She was right. Having recently been burned by both of my parents, trust was not something I was ready to give away freely. Plus, I was concerned I'd make a lousy husband. The only role model I had in that department dumped all over his wife for the better part of twenty-five years. And what if things didn't work out between Lara and me? I couldn't risk the possibility that I might follow in my father's path to self-destruction.

"Um... I can't. Not yet. I just need a little more time to mourn my dad," I replied. If I told her the truth, that I was afraid to get married, she would probably leave me.

Her lips formed the words, "That's okay," but her body language and actions suggested otherwise. In the coming weeks and months, our time spent together involved little physical interaction and a good deal of forced conversation.

Since returning from Vancouver, the only thing I did that made any sense was my enrollment in a writing class with a teacher by the name of Matt Hoverman. I still had no idea what I was going to write about and if this class didn't work out, I would probably get a return visit from an angry Ghost Dad, who had not appeared since the Japanese garden.

The first day of class was held at a midtown Manhattan dance rehearsal studio in a building that looked like an old sweatshop, only recently divided up with makeshift walls. Up eight flights and at the end of a long hallway was Matt, the teacher, peering out of a doorway. He was balder than his picture from the website and smiled menacingly, his eyebrows moving up and down while he waved from a distance.

Something about the way this scene was playing out did not feel right. It reminded me of the time when I was nineteen years old and took a meeting in a New Jersey forest with a man who called himself a film director.

HALF-MAN. HALF-MONKEY. HALF INCREDIBLY NAIVE.

The year was 2003. The Iraq War began and French fries became known as Freedom Fries. I had just moved out of my parents' house and was desperate to make a name for myself as a professional actor.

In late fall, while trolling Craigslist for casting notices, I saw a posting for a new film set in a post-apocalyptic New Jersey. It was starring a few no-name up-and-coming professional wrestlers and it paid a few hundred dollars.

I answered the ad with a picture and resume and got a phone call from the director who sounded like he had a cold. He said I was "perfect for the role of a half-man, half-monkey who runs the prison that holds the wrestlers and then goes crazy."

"Awesome. I was born for this role." I was as earnest as I was green.

"I need you to meet me in North Jersey at the Dover train station near my mother's house. We'll discuss the film a bit more and how you fit in."

Later that week I got on a train to go to North Jersey to meet with this director. When I got there, I was met by a man who was pockmarked, a little glassy-eyed, and had a mullet. He never spoke above a loud whisper.

"Nice to meet you, Joshua. We're going to take a ride to Minisink County Park where we're going film the m-m-m-movie," the mullet-man said with a nervous stutter.

(—D-d-d-don't do this, dawg. He's gonna try to put it in you.—)

(—Don't be silly. He's in show business.—)

Despite my hesitations, the car ride wasn't too bad. We talked about my career aspirations as an actor. We even spoke about his wrestler friends who were going to be in his movie and how he got into filmmaking.

When we arrived at the park, he suggested that we take a walk deep into the forest and we did.

And it was there he told me it was time to audition for the film.

"Ok, Josh, basically your character is half-man and half-monkey and goes nuts in the film, because he loves the taste of human flesh," he said while licking his crusty white lips. "So here's what we're going to do. I'm going to get on the ground and lay down and you have to get on top of me and pretend that you're eating my face off and ripping away my body parts, and you have to be convincing."

"Can't I just do a monologue?" I asked, my stranger-danger alert now kicking into high gear.

"No!" he replied, exasperated that I would ask such a ridiculous question. "It has to be this. I need to see if you can handle this—see if you have the chops for it."

He got on the ground and lay on his back, closed his eyes, and a little smile came across his face. And I thought to myself, "Man, this is weird as shit... but I want to be in a film with wrestlers."

So I got on the ground and pretended to gnaw at his face and rip away his body parts and went to town on that dude for about five minutes.

When I finished he thanked me and said I did a great job. He even took me to Friendly's for some

Rocky Road and then sent me back to the train station. While on the train going home I was happy with how the day went until I got to the Elizabeth stop when I realized he was never going to call me.

And he never did. I still wonder to this day if that guy is on a sex offender list somewhere.

First-Day Jitters

As I continued my walk down the long hallway, Matt's creepy eyebrow movement stopped. He invited me into the classroom with a hearty handshake and a warm hello. With that and the sight of a few friendly faces, students already in the room sitting at a long folding table, my fear of being given an unwanted rectal exam was subdued.

For our first order of business, Matt had each student sitting around the table introduce themselves. There was John, an older gentleman, also a teacher who happened to be a dead ringer for Colonel Sanders. Aaron was a twenty-something guy whose eyes were red and glazed over—like a transplant from an early 1990's Lollapalooza concert. Then there was Mary, a boisterous and heavyset woman with an infectious laugh who made her living as a stand-up comedian. And finally there was PJ, a physically fit freckled man of Irish decent wearing a T-shirt that said NAVY. He also made a living as a stand-up comedian.

Matt had each of us tell an amusing or embarrassing story about ourselves or someone we knew. Colonel Sanders, Lollapalooza Guy, and the two comedians all went before me, each telling a tale of the amusing variety. Not to be outdone, I decided to tell my "Cocoa Pebbles" story—a chilling account of hunger, unrequited love, and rancid diarrhea.

COCOA PEBBLES AND THE ONE THAT GOT AWAY

Right after high school my friend Hsoj and I got cast in a community theatre production of *Joseph and the Amazing Technicolor Dreamcoat* in Asbury Park, New Jersey. In between a matinee and an evening performance, I, Hsoj, and our new friend Mike got hungry and bored, so we all took a long walk to a sandwich shop where we each bought a greasy, fatty, foot-long cheesesteak and an extra-large soda.

Shortly after finishing our meals, the three of us played around for a little bit on the boardwalk until Hsoj's metabolism went into overdrive, causing all the meat and soda he just consumed to run through him like a chocolate river. The closest place that was open that had a public restroom was at the theater in which we were performing.

After a mad and labored dash back to the theater, Hsoj was stricken with terror because the theater was locked and there were no other open buildings in sight. Desperate, Hsoj climbed a ladder along the side of the building and onto a balcony that had an entrance into the theater. But that door was locked as well. Sweating and swearing, Hsoj climbed up two more stories but each time was denied entry by a locked door. When Hsoj got to the very top of the building, he couldn't hold it in anymore and relieved himself on a pile of brown pebbles. He could only clean his underside with a few pieces of stray cardboard that he was fortunate were casually lying around.

Embarrassed and ashamed, Hsoj begged us not to tell anyone about what had just occurred. But later in the day, Hsoj found out that Mike had thought it would be funnier to take some of our cast mates, including a girl that Hsoj liked, on a tour to the top of the building to show them his brown masterpiece. For a whole month, Hsoj was affectionately known to our cast mates as "Cocoa Pebbles." The girl that Hsoj liked felt so much pity toward him that she bought him a roll of Scott Tissue and never spoke to him again.

LESSONS IN STORYTELLING

By the time I finished my story, my teacher and classmates were all grimacing, their collective gaze affixed to the ground. Following a brief awkward silence, PJ snickered like a frat boy, slapped his knee, and yelled out, "Dude, Hsoj was totally you." I'm pretty sure everyone else had already beaten him to that conclusion. With "Cocoa Pebbles" I learned an important and timeless truth: All poop stories are not created equal, mine falling in the categories of "unfunny" and "painfully embarrassing." My first attempt at telling a story in front of an audience was an epic flop and I wanted nothing more than to crawl into a dark hole forever, safe from Ghost Dad who would surely come to visit me that very same night as a result of my poor performance in class.

Just before the end of class, Matt assigned homework. We were required to read a packet on the basics of storytelling, then write a one-page version of our life story, which we would read aloud during the next class. That week, every second of my free time was spent creating multiple versions of my father's life story which I could pass off as my own.

For my first attempt, I spun a little yarn about all the girls from his diary, including Holly, the coffee shop girl, and a few elementary school crushes. But it felt disingenuous and bit too Oedipal, so I scrapped it halfway into the week.

On my second attempt, I pieced together a story about all the jobs he had ever held: substitute teacher, department store clerk, and his thirty-year run at the New Jersey Department of Environmental Protection. However, I was afraid that this version would spark a worldwide contagion of narcolepsy, so I trashed it the night before the assignment was due.

(—*A nighttime vengeance is mine, sayeth your father.*—)

(—*Your pops is gonna be pissed, you don't get something written.*—)

(—*No sleeping for you tonight, papi. Eres un puto!*—)

Because Lara had to make it to her office job by 8 a.m., I couldn't burn the midnight oil in our living room slash bedroom. So I made our bathroom into my makeshift office.

The first hour was spent trying to figure out whether it was more comfortable to sit on the toilet or the floor. The second hour was a quiet reflection on whether I should sit on the toilet with lid up or down. Into the third hour, I gave up completely on the toilet idea and sat in the tub with my computer, frustrated to the point of muted whimpering by my lack of progress. But it was in the comfort of the cool, porcelain half-shell of my bathtub that words spilled effortlessly from my fingers and onto the computer screen.

This story was not about my father after all. Most of it was about the difficulties I had growing up a wannabe movie star in a fundamentalist home ruled by a despot named Doug. It had the makings of a masterpiece—self-deprecating humor, show business, suicide, and ten-point single-spaced Times New Roman font with margins that nearly stretched beyond the width of the entire page.

The following evening during our class show-and-tell, Colonel Sanders, Mary, PJ, and even Lollapalooza Guy all gave brave, somber, and humorous retellings of their life stories that involved Oreo cookies, Filipino drill sergeants, network television, and a cantankerous old English teacher.

Finally it was my turn, but the fervor I felt about what I had written in my bathtub dissipated into nausea and fear. I'd never confessed anything so intimate to anyone, much less a group of strangers. And there was a strong possibility that this could be an even bigger pile of manure than the "Cocoa Pebbles" story.

As I walked to the front of the class, my hand clutched tightly to the script I was about to read as if my kung fu grip was going to save me from the self-inflicted and public humiliation I was about to endure.

"I began my life as a winner. I beat out all the other little sperm; yes, I was the one who made contact with the egg."

(—*You hear that? It's the sound of crickets, bitch. You ain't funny.*—)

(—Shut up. I would be if they were standing in my bathroom last night.—)

I was totally bombing, and pulling a Michael Richards was not an option, so I clutched even harder to my script and sped through the rest, barely breathing, never looking up from the page. As my eyes reached the finish line, that final period on the page, I detected the sound of sympathy applause coming from the teacher and three of my classmates. Apparently Lollapalooza Guy got up while I was reading. He never did come back. That was his last class.

I hurried back to my seat with my head down, preparing myself for some harsh criticism from Matt and the rest of my fellow burgeoning wordsmiths.

"How are you feeling, Josh?" Matt asked.

I hesitated and took a few deep breaths to calm the frantic pace at which my heart was beating.

"Um, my stomach hurts a little and I might be having a mild heart attack, but I'm doing okay. I was scared up there, but I think I might be running on some kind of adrenaline right now. I feel... good... good. Better."

"Dude, I loved the part about the deaf guy asking about your mom having big-headed children. Hilarious," said PJ.

"I really liked the part about how you were a glorified tackling dummy on your high school football team," said Mary with a cackle.

"I thought the part where you talked about your father's suicide was absolutely courageous," said Colonel Sanders.

Though their praise was a bit compulsory, their kind words renewed an artistic energy inside of me that I had forgotten existed. Having spent the last few years getting beaten down and rejected at hundreds of auditions, I couldn't remember the last time anyone had said something good about my creative work.

During this introductory writing course, Matt taught us the finer points on how to properly structure a story. Outside of class, I lived and breathed everything related to writing and the art of the solo-play. I began experimenting with my own writing style, drawing up short scenes that could be integrated into the play I would write for my dead father. On days that I didn't feel particularly creative, I would sit in coffee shops just so I could catch a whiff of a freshly brewed nutty dark roast while watching scores of future Ernest Hemingways and Virginia Woolfs hard at work.

This four-week class brought about some pretty remarkable things as well. Firstly, I had stopped, at least for the time being, having nightly visits from

Ghost Dad, which quieted the questions I had about my sanity. Secondly, I had started to understand my father a bit better by writing about him, quelling much of my anger and resentment toward him. And lastly, Matt offered me entrance into his premier Level Two writing course where I could piece together all of my short stories from the Level One course into a fully functional one-man show.

RIVEDAL V. RIVEDAL, ROUND: 2

In September and in between writing classes another remarkable—no, miraculous—thing happened. My family's house was sold. This was the house that I helped build with my own two hands as a twelve-year-old boy; the house that kept me from sleeping on the floor of a one-bedroom apartment in Trenton, New Jersey; the house with the shoddy craftsmanship and the unsightly cornflower blue siding; the house that should not have sold in what was a buyer's market; the house from which I stood to gain a profit; and the house that was the last formal tie I had to my mother.

As soon as I got word of the sale from my sister, I rented an SUV and drove down to spend a day clearing out my old trophies, drawings, and child-hood belongings while trying to avoid my mother like a case of the mumps. Later that week, Holly sent me a text message telling me she loved me and asking if she could expect Lara and me for Thanksgiving. I responded to her through email.

Holly,

I would like you to do me a favor. Please stop tex-ting me and telling me you love me. I don't need your love. I need an apology from you to ever con-sider us having a relationship ever again. As it stands, I am completely okay not having a rela-tionship with you even if you did apologize.

I don't know how you can live with yourself after the crap you pulled.

I was forced to go get a lawyer because you were contesting what your, by all means, ex-husband left to his children—YOUR children. You tried to take everything away from us but your own greed blew up in your face. You are lucky you have nice chil-dren because if we wanted to we could have gone in that courtroom and left you with next to nothing.

What's sad is that this to me was never about the money. I wanted the funeral to be taken care of. I wanted to see you be a little more comfortable, but anything in excess of that wasn't necessary because this money was nothing any of us earned. It's blood money.

You've allowed yourself to become an ugly, bitter, and self-deluded person.

You've had months to apologize and haven't felt the impetus to do so. And I won't take my Thanksgiving to visit you so you can bullshit me in New Jersey. I may consider having a dialogue with you if you apologize and admit what you did was wrong, but until then, no more texts about how you love me. If you loved me, we wouldn't be having this conversation.

Josh

The antagonistic tone of my message, reminiscent of the vitriol between two angry high school cheerleaders fighting over the same boy, got my mother's attention. She wrote back immediately and said she was willing to meet up with me in New York City any time so we could talk.

I wasn't prepared for that kind of response. I thought she was going to fight me tooth and nail and we'd have a battle royal the likes of which Gmail and Sweet Valley High had never seen. After a few days of my own introspective radio silence, I decided to meet with her, but only because our feud was affecting my relationship with my brother, who stopped returning my calls. He didn't understand how I "could treat our mother so badly," and didn't want to associate with me.

We met on a weekday in mid-January. I chose a Starbucks near Penn Station in Manhattan as our rendezvous point. I figured her aversion to coffee would keep our meeting short. I arrived first and sat at a table on the second floor of the venti-sized coffee shop. As she walked up the stairs to greet me, her eyes locked with mine, her countenance inscrutable. When on the top step, she opened her arms to hug me, a surprising move which I sidestepped.

"Have a seat. I know you had some things you wanted to say in response to my email. Now is the time to say them," I launched in, wasting no time with pleasantries.

"I felt hurt by what you wrote to me. And I felt you were disrespectful in the way you called me by my first name."

(—*You're mad lucky you weren't called anything worse.*—)

I presented my opening arguments. "You have to give respect to get respect. Lying to me not once, but twice, was disrespectful and it hurt me."

(—*Let the record show, papito. Today is your day in court, coño!*—)

"I'm sorry. I was wrong for that. And if I ever caused you any pain or heartache—I never wanted to do anything like that. I'm your mother and I love you," she said, pleading her paper-thin argument.

(—*Love is kind. Love is patient. Love is gentle. Love does not lie...*—)

"I hear you say that but I have a hard time believing you." I wasn't going to fall for the old "I'm your mother" pity defense.

"It's true. I remember holding you in my arms as a baby—"

"I don't want to hear about that. I want to know why you had to take your children to court. You didn't have to do that."

(—*Preach, brother. Turn the lights on!*—)
(—*¡Si, papi, si!*—)
(—*Say it! Say it loud! I'm black and I'm proud.*—)
(—*Too far.*—)

"I am working on my life. I have made some mistakes and I made one here with you. I'm sorry.

Can you please ever forgive me? I love you so much," she said, the tears forming at the corners of her eyes.

I had no idea whether the words she spoke were genuine. But a crying woman never fails to warm my heart, whether it be a little girl who fell and skinned her knee, Leona Helmsley, or a sworn adversary. My mother's warm tears cut through my bitter, cold heart.

"I, um... I can forgive you," I said. I was shocked that those words actually were coming out of my mouth. "I don't know if I love you or want to have a relationship with you. But... I think I need to forgive you. I won't forget this, but I forgive you."

Our transaction now complete, I told her I had to leave for a last-minute audition, which wasn't true. I just didn't want to be in the same room as her any longer than I had to be. We hugged and I walked the forty blocks uptown back to my apartment. The weight of this grudge I had been holding toward my mother had gotten heavier as the months passed and became a burden much too difficult to bear. The words of forgiveness I offered, though not a total absolution for her or for me, lightened my load, making just enough room for me, the voices, Ghost Dad, show business, marriage anxiety, and my continued long-term fruitless pursuit of happiness.

TWENTY

....

REPENT, THE END IS NIGH

After my mother made official her intention to divorce my father in August of 2008, I started writing in a diary once a day. I used it to vent off some steam about the further deterioration of the perfect family for whom I had always wished. That diary soon turned into the script for a seven-character play loosely based on my family called *It's Good to be Home*. I tooled around with this script in my spare time until just before my father's death.

In fall 2009, while on the audition circuit, I made the acquaintance of a well-spoken but twitchy young actor, Phil, who ran a small New York theatre company looking for new play-scripts. Hoping for a producer with access to an audience for my new and unfinished one-man show, I pressed Phil into listening to my long and drawn out description of what I thought this one-man play would eventually become—a story of religious freedom, The Great White Chocolate (me), and a love/hate affair with my father followed by his untimely death.

"That sounds pretty good," said Phil, following a pregnant pause filled with deep thought and a good deal of tugging on his fat lower lip, "but what I *really* need is an original multi-person play I can develop from scratch."

I offered up *It's Good to be Home* as an appetizer to the promise of future development for my untitled one-man play and so Phil could realize his dream of embodying his idol, Lee Strasburg, the Jew who saved ensemble theatre, much like the Jew who once saved all the future Christians. Our marriage of convenience came with two other caveats: I had to appear as an actor in another one of their plays, and I had to lend money to his theatre company.

THE STING OF FAILURE

Following a month of development on *It's Good to be Home*, which included incessant requests from Phil that I retool the script, my original storyline became almost unrecognizable. It started out as the cautionary tale of a mildly successful art gallery owner who steals millions of dollars from his mother and dying father. But after Phil stuck his imperious little hand into the script, it became the story of a popular gay New York City actor who dupes his family out of an oil reserve on a piece of land they all owned together in Western Pennsylvania.

Phil, who thought we were on the right track with the script, scheduled a public reading of the play on a Sunday night in mid-December with a cast of actors so I could hear what wasn't working with the script and make the necessary changes. We had promises from more than twenty people, many of them members of Phil's theatre company. Only four people showed. The only comment I got from the audience was from a plump and elfin-looking elderly man who eagerly pulled me aside to tell me my writing was "the disingenuous work of an amateur, only fixable after a decade's worth of rewrites."

I went home that night with no discernible clues as to how to fix the script, my first crack at professional playwriting a total disaster. I was disappointed that I didn't trust my instincts while developing this piece. Letting Phil seize near complete control of the project and script turned it into an unlikable and pretentious piece of drivel. I couldn't bear to look at it ever again and placed it on top of my bookshelf behind some old textbooks.

So as to not wake my blond sleeping beauty in the next room, I sat in my bathtub in a pool of sorrow accompanied by two bottles of Pinot Noir to numb the sting of insults hurled by the elderly elf-in man.

(—*You were an idiot for even trying, pendajo.*—)

(—*Honkey, you should quit that writing class too.*—)

(—You're right. I'm just going to embarrass myself again.—)

A full week after the death of *It's Good to Be Home*, life returned to the doldrums prior to my Vancouver trip. Late one night while commiserating in my watering hole slash bathtub with two new bottles of Pinot Noir, an alluring pair of medium-bodied consolatory confidants, I tried to work up the courage to call Matt. I wanted to tell him I was going to drop his class. Just before popping the cork on my second bottle of wine, I laid my head back to rest my eyes and fell sound asleep. Once more, I found myself in a very familiar rainforest.

TWENTY-ONE

························

DROWNING IN UNFINISHED BUSINESS

The lush vegetation and bright green canopy had changed. Once rich and full of life, it was now tinted in shades of brown and red, withered from drought and disease. The sun shone brightly on the horizon and within moments it shot up to its apex. Its rays were so hot they burned my skin, causing it to droop off of my body. I tried to jump down into the ravine to swim in the river at its base, but my feet had melted into the ground.

"Help! Somebody help me," I screamed while flapping my sagging arms like wings. I was terrified that I would die a painful death if I couldn't move or at least wake up. As I let out another loud shriek, the moon came into view and eclipsed the sun. At a glance, my skin and feet had returned to normal. In front of me, and floating a few inches off the ground, my dead father appeared.

"You have to continue. You have to keep going," he said. His face was expressionless.

"I can't. You have to find somebody else... "It has to be you."

"But it's difficult and I'm no good and it hurts," I said, now in tears.

"You'll get better. You have to keep going," he said as he placed his hand on my shoulder to comfort me.

I wanted to embrace him in a hug, but my arms wouldn't move. In an instant, it began to rain. I looked up for just a second so I could feel the cool drops of water falling on my face, but when I looked back down my father was gone.

It didn't take long for the rain to rage into a monsoon that had now flooded the ravine and what was once the rainforest. The water rose above my head and I had to swim with all of my might just to avoid drowning. The harder I paddled my arms and legs, the more violent the storm grew. Waves more than fifty feet tall were now crashing over me. I fought hard to keep my head above the surface, but a strong current pulled me under. As the water began to fill my lungs, I abruptly woke from my sleep coughing and choking on saliva that had gone down the wrong tube in my throat.

TWENTY-TWO

....

A J-RIZZLE JOINT™

The next morning I sat in front of my computer fighting off a nasty hangover while trying to find the inspiration to continue composing my and my father's story. Two hours, one aspirin, and three cups of coffee put my hangover into a sleeper hold. Soon enough I had written a new scene—a much needed sliver of success.

NARRATOR JOSH
Though we had nothing else in common, music was something we almost bonded over. One year, my father decided he wanted to buy a bunch of old Ed Sullivan videotapes. He would sit and watch them over and over again. One day I wandered in while he was watching and started asking questions.

KID JOSH
(Enamored with what's on the TV)
Dad, who are these people? Are they Christians? Why is that man moving around like
that? Why is that lady so shiny? Can I watch
this too?

DAD
These were some of the greatest performers of
all time. They're inspirational. And if you want
to watch this with me you can't tell anyone
about it at church. Now sit down and shut up.

NARRATOR JOSH
So, I sat down and I shut up and he and I
watched those tapes all the way through. We
didn't say anything to each other. We didn't
fight or yell. We just sat there and watched, and
boy, was I mesmerized. It was the first time I
had seen anything other than Christian performers or Christian music and it was amazing.

There was a young Elvis Presley swinging and
moving his hips to "Hound Dog." There were
the Beatles singing "Ticket to Ride." There was
the legendary Ella Fitzgerald and Sammy Da-
vis Jr. in duet singing "S'wonderful." There
was the Rolling Stones, Johnny Mathis, Bobby
Darin, productions of Camelot, My Fair Lady,

West Side Story, the distinct comedic stylings of Moms Mabley—

MOM'S MABLEY
(An old toothless comedienne)
The other night my mother came home with a man, and now he's living with us. He was a puny, crusty, moldy old man. He's so old Santa Claus looks like his son. He's older than his mother. And ugly! Honest to goodness he was so ugly he hurt my feelings. I told him the other night that one of us has got to die because I can't put up with him.

NARRATOR JOSH
What a performer, what a pioneer. And let's not forget about The Byrds, Harry Belafonte, The Doors getting banned for singing "Light My Fire"—this was the sixties, people—Eartha Kitt, The Smothers Brothers, Nat King Cole, Louis Armstrong, The Supremes, The Jackson Five. There was even the Italian mouse puppet Topo Gigio who would come out at the end of the show and say—

TOPO GIGIO
(A high-pitched Italian accent)
Eddie, before I go to sleep... kiss me goodnight ha-ha-ha!!

NARRATOR JOSH

Through all of that my father and I just sat there in silence watching those brilliant performers. And after it was over we both looked up and looked at each other for a second, each of us wanting to describe how we felt about what we just saw. But nothing was said and we both looked away, got up, and never spoke about it again.

Yet somehow I knew that seeing the Ed Sullivan Show changed my life forever. I was inspired. I wanted to be just like Robert Goulet, so I decided that I was going to go out for the sixth grade school musical...

The finale of Matt's advanced writing class provided an opportunity for me and my classmates to read and act out a twenty-minute portion of our new solo-shows in front of a live and paying audience. Matt saw this component as a confidence booster for the performer and a way to bring their stories to life, but I found it daunting—another opportunity to be judged an amateur.

I needed to come up with a title for my one-man play as part of this public showing. After tossing around winners like *Josh's Magic Fun-Time Hour,* and

A *J-Rizzle Joint,* I chose *Not the Hemingways* in a nod to one of the final lines in the script.

The night of our big class recital, the forty-seat theater in which the event was being held was overcapacity. Audience members had to stand along the aisles and in the doorway.

(*—Papi, vamos. You're gonna make a fool of yourself ...—*)

(*—Go 'head, dawg. You just like your pops anyway...—*)

(—You're right. I can't do this. I've gotta get the hell out of here.—)

But every available exit was blocked and I was stuck. Before I knew it, Matt had finished giving my introduction and I was on stage reading my script at a mile a minute. At some point near the beginning and in between quick breaths, I heard what I thought was laughter coming from the audience. So I slowed down to see if I could hear more. And in that moment that audience and I began to have something that resembled an intimate conversation. We laughed, reminisced, and even cried together. As the lights went down and then back up, I took a bow and the sound of applause roared through the crowd. I got what I thought was a standing ovation, but it turned out to be two women in the middle of the back row who needed to leave for the bathroom. Still, the reading was a bigger success than I ever imagined. That night while asleep, I found myself in the rainforest.

TWENTY-THREE

IT'S A BIRD... IT'S A PLANE... IT'S GHOST DAD

I t had regained its verdurous canopy since my last visit. The sun was positioned at two o'clock. Not yet at its brightest point, it was partially hidden by two fluffy white clouds. I looked across the ravine and into the endless barren desert directly across from me. With no Ghost Dad in sight, I began to walk into the rainforest in case he found his way in.

I didn't take more than three steps before a fierce gust of wind blew me over. As I returned to my feet and brushed myself off, from out of the corner of my eye I spotted the tail end of an object flying through the sky. But all I could see was what looked like long hair flowing behind it like the tail of a comet. It was him. I tried to pivot my head as fast as I could but was unable to catch up to his speed. When I fully turned again to face the desert, I looked up to the sky to see if my phantom father would return, but he didn't. All he left behind was a trail of large puffy white capital letters that said KEEP GOING.

TWENTY-FOUR

....

SIX ORDERS OF THE GOSPEL

I told a room of more than forty people his story. Wasn't that enough for this self-aggrandizing ghost? And how was I supposed to "keep going"? Class was over and I didn't know anyone who was interested in developing and producing a partially completed one-man show except Phil, and I wasn't going to let him or his theatre company strangle the life out of another one of my plays.

A few days after our class reading, Matt sent out information about a few play festivals looking for one-person shows. He said it was possible they would give his students preferential treatment.

Perhaps through one of these festivals I would find the magic formula to exorcise my dead father once and for all.

There were two big festivals to which I could apply, the International Fringe and the Midtown International Theatre Festival, both in New York City. Each would take at least six weeks to hear back from and each commenced nearly half a year away in July and August respectively. I didn't know if I could wait that long to regain my sanity, but it was worth a try.

Just prior to sending in my application, I thought it would be better to change the name of the play from *Not the Hemingways* to *The Gospel According to Josh*. The latter seemed like a more provocative choice and one that would help set my play apart from the thousands of other applicants.

With all of my I's dotted and T's crossed, I sent off my applications and put my hope and trust in the hands of the good people at the United States Postal Service. Time to play the waiting game.

(—*You gotta put your aspirations in check, homeslice.*—)

(—*What happens when the show doesn't get in, amigo? Suici...*—)

(—No! I just need sleep...—)

(—*To every thing there is a season. A time to die.*—)

(—No. No. Not yet.—)

Eight weeks later, I opened my mailbox to find a letter from the New York International Fringe Festival who had finally had gotten back to me with their response.

(*—Papi, no lo abra. Do. Not. Open. It's gonna be bad news.—*)

I carefully tore open the letter while walking from my mailbox and back inside to my apartment.

(*—You is a magnet for bad news, dawg.—*)

```
Thanking you for applying. We were
overwhelmed by the thousands of ap-
plicants. Regrettably we can only
choose about two hundred of them...
```

(—What is wrong with me? Even these assholes don't want me.—)

```
...We do want to invite you to apply
next year.
```

A very generous offer.

(*—Those bitches.—*)

That night, and after a bottle of wine and a good cry at my tavern slash bathtub slash part-time office, I was visited by my dead father who again instructed me via skywriting to KEEP GOING.

I still had one last shot with the Midtown International Theatre Festival, who got back to me through email a few days after getting rejected by the Fringe. Wanting to avoid the sting of another failure, it took me nearly half of a week to open the email. One night, at the end of a twelve-hour workday and after a few ounces of liquid courage found at a neighborhood pub, I stumbled home. Bracing myself on the railing of my front porch, I opened the festival's email on my smartphone.

```
The Midtown International Theatre
Festival would be honored if you
would produce THE GOSPEL ACCORDING TO
JOSH in this year's festival. We
would like to give you an 80-min.
time slot in the Dorothy Strelsin
Theatre for 6 performances. Please e-
mail notification of acceptance as
soon as possible.
```

I had to reread that email several times mostly because I was drunk but also to make sure they were actually saying "yes." It was a very surreal moment in my life, like one of those happy yet rare instances on the elementary school playground when I wasn't picked last for a game of basketball. Somebody actually wanted me and it didn't take death or a legal battle for them to express it.

Everything I had set out to do with my father's money, albeit blood money, I was doing—I was writing, I got to travel, I dove into the exciting world of retirement planning for myself, and I even got headshots that made me look like a man.

PARTY OF ONE

With this newfound professional success and the extra workload that came with *The Gospel According to Josh,* I was left little room for anything else in my life. The price I paid for this was loneliness. I still couldn't tell anyone about my dreams, afraid I would be permanently branded as a "lunatic," so I continued to keep them to myself. I even canceled plans to see my family for Christmas and Thanksgiving that year just to avoid my mother. Not wanting to lose Lara, I kept her close physically, but at a distance emotionally. And I started to lose touch with what few friends I had. The only steady companions I could manage to keep was the Ghost formerly known as Douglas and the triumvirate of voices who were now mostly coming to visit late at night when all else was quiet. They plied booze and pot, and frequent discussion as to whether self-death was to be a fate inherited from my father.

I was not sure how long I could last like this, but the beginning of the end was near and somewhere out there was a straw waiting to break this camel's back.

TWENTY-FIVE

....

THE GHOST, THE NOTEBOOK, AND THE CRAYON

In the months leading up to the professional New York festival debut of *The Gospel According to Josh*, the Adonis Viking, that ghost of my dead father, continued to pillage my dreams on a weekly basis with the simple instruction to KEEP GOING. One night, however, his message changed.

He appeared directly in front of me and floated a few feet off the ground, still not able to set foot in the rainforest for reasons he would not or perhaps could not explain.

"Take another look at your mission," he said with an uncharacteristic sense of urgency in his voice. "The notebook. The crayon."

"I'm doing everything you wanted me to do."

"There's more."

"I can't," I said firmly.

"You must. The notebook and the red crayon."

And with that, he blew a powerful stream of wind right in my face that caused me to wake from my sleep. The screen on my alarm clock flashed 8 a.m. and it was time to start my day.

TWENTY-SIX

....

THE CAMEL AND THE CALM
BEFORE THE STRAW

A notebook and red crayon? Why wouldn't he give me a break? I was afraid if I disobeyed he might start making visits while my eyes were open while singing at an audition or riding the 6 train. So I went over to the dresser where I had placed the notebook that listed in red crayon everything I was going to do with my father's inheritance money. Scanning the scrawl of that to-do list, there was one item I'd forgotten about and still hadn't crossed off—finish my college education.

The three-year absence of an acting career led me to restaurant work, an occupation that: was flexible enough that I could still go to auditions, required no formal education, and made me feel like a stupid and substandard human being. Customers can treat waiters like a crusty dog turd stuck to the bottom of their shoes because:

a) They simply fancy watching you squirm.

b) They had a terrible day and have no one else to verbally pummel because their spouse is out of town with the family dog *and* the family goldfish.

c) The customer is always right. The sun revolves around the earth. Babies come from kissing. Gay people cause earthquakes. And you, Garçon Joshua, have the brain capacity of an underdeveloped Neanderthal.

d) They swear to G-d and on the grave of their "favorite great-uncle Morrie" that they told you to leave the chickpeas, onions, feta cheese, croutons, celery, and red peppers out of their salad because they're "deathly allergic to anything that casts a shadow."

But a college degree could get me some damn respect, along with a one-way ticket out of the hospitality industry forever. What would I do to make money? Teaching? I was good with kids and could be the cool high school English teacher who all the other teachers wanted to be and who all the students wanted to be with. My wardrobe? Wool turtlenecks and blazers with patches on the elbows. With teaching I could work till three, perform in a Broadway show at night, and have my summers off. I'd be Morgan Freeman from *Lean on Me* during the day and regular actor Morgan Freeman at night. Sweet! I love Morgan Freeman. I had to tip my hat to Ghost Dad in thanks for the reminder about college.

A return to school would require grueling and cerebral work and exceptional discipline to relearn the complex language of academia. I was already juggling so many things that throwing one more flaming sword into the mix did not really seem that absurd. Hell, a dead person was even encouraging it. The other upside to finishing college, besides a handsome new mortar board, was that the more work I took on the less I would have to deal with the pressure of unwanted wedding bells, the voices, and the questions about my familial legacy. Within a few weeks I applied to Baruch College in New York City.

Within a month, I got my acceptance letter in the mail. A math placement test awaited me, which I swiftly failed with flying colors. This landed my mathematically-impaired backside in a summer remedial college algebra course.

Days were spent waiting tables, memorizing lines, studying parabolas and the Pythagorean theorem, and hustling to sell tickets to *The Gospel According to Josh*. There was no time for despair, only the task directly in front of me. Theatre producer, writer, actor, and college student—thankfully I was born with an abnormally large head to accommodate all the hats I was wearing.

IF I CAN MAKE IT THERE, I'LL MAKE IT ANYWHERE...

While wearing my theatre producer cap, I was able to score a bit of good luck. While sending out show invites on Facebook, I found and secured the attendance of two Broadway producers to my show. In the event that this festival production wasn't enough for the media hungry Ghost Dad, I had no doubt that these two producers would help extend the life of the show after the six scheduled performances came to a close.

It was now opening night of *The Gospel According to Josh* in the Theatre Capital of the World. While nervously pacing in my dressing room, twenty minutes prior to showtime, I got a buzz from my smartphone notifying me that I had a fresh batch of emails.

The first message was from one of the Broadway producers who had to cancel his ticket to take "a last-minute vacation because of job stress." I restrained myself from responding with the hope that he'd get struck with a serious case of E. Coli and have the worst vacation of his life.

The second email was from my mother who told me she was coming to see my show later in the week. I hadn't spoken to her since our reconciliatory rendezvous at Starbucks in January. She must've heard about the show through my withered grapevine of sibling chatter. The thought of having my mother in the audience made me rather anxious. I did a full-on bad impersonation of her in the show and my script had a few four-letter words and a p-word that sometimes ends with "cats" or "willows."

The third email was from the second Broadway producer who also had to cancel his ticket. His elderly mother had recently been admitted to a hospital out on Long Island where he would stay, indefinitely, to help nurse her back to good health.

(—*Homeboy, you can't catch a break. You ain't gonna to cry, are you?*—)

"Please unwrap all candies and turn off all cell phones," a festival staff member implored the audience from the stage. "And without further ado, *The Gospel According to Josh.*"

(—*Pendajo, your dad won't be happy about this.*—)
(—*And there shall be weeping and gnashing of teeth...*—)
(—Shut up! I still have a show to do! God!—)

With all lights in the theater now completely dark and with glow tape as my only guide, I walked out of my dressing room and to a black stool in the middle of the stage where I sat completely still until two spotlights were turned on—my cue to start the show.

"O-B-E-D-I-E-N-C-E. OBEDIENCE IS THE VERY BEST WAY TO SHOW THAT YOU BELIEVE," I sang, playing the role of an overly enthusiastic kindergarten Sunday school teacher.

That first show was spent entirely in my head and in survival mode. Somehow I got through that six-minute show on some sort of primitive instinctual autopilot.

After I took my final bow, a bushy-haired middle-aged man with muttonchops for side burns darted toward me to shake my hand. He could have been Karl Marx' great-grandson. "Our life stories are so interrelated." The rest of his words were drowned out by an obtuse and obnoxiously loud conversation from the back corner of the theater between two older women, cackling on about how my father was "a bastard" who "could've asked for help" but didn't because "he deserved to die."

Finishing up my one-sided conversation with the bushy haired man, I hustled back to my dressing room to regroup after performing what was an emotionally draining show.

POKING THE MONSTER

While changing back into my civilian clothing I couldn't help but mull over the cruel things the two cackling ladies had said about my father. Were they right about him? Could he have gotten help? What if he had tried and I wasn't listening? What if the sleeping pills and the suicide note were a cry for help gone terribly wrong?

That night, while Lara was fast asleep, while on my computer and under the fluorescent lighting of my bathroom slash office slash pub, I started to type into Google "kinds of people who commit sui—"

(—*Mira, coñaso, they're just going to have a picture of you.*—)

(—That's what I'm scared of. But... I can't just...—)

(—*What? Leave this alone? Idle hands are the devil's workshop. Suicide...*—)

(—No. No! I'm just a little sad. And curious... No!—)

Whatever sort of devil that lived beyond those search results could very well have been the same one that killed my father. Was it now also hunting me? I couldn't provoke that monster any further. I couldn't finish typing the word "suicide" into Google.

The rest of the six-show run of *The Gospel According to Josh* went better than I could've ever imagined. My performance improved each night, as did the size of my audiences. The shows my brother and sister attended were two of my very best. Though I never told them about Ghost Dad's visits, afraid my sanity would become the subject of a public trial with a jury of my kin, I was excited to show them what I had been working on in the aftermath of our father's death. My brother came with five of his friends and laughed the loudest and applauded the hardest out of everyone in the theater. He didn't have much to say about it other than he enjoyed it, but his visit and support put our relationship back on track. My sister sat in the front row and watched expressionless, save for the few times she smiled at my impressions of people from our childhood. After the show was over, we hugged, released a few tears, and said, "I love you," to each other. I wasn't nearly as comfortable having my mother come see my work. I censored all of the swear words and I felt my acting work became bland and subdued. But after the show she was very complimentary. "You looked happy up there. You're doing good work." Good work, maybe. Happy, not so much.

No Broadway producers ever came to see the show. However, due to a prior friendship with staff at The Media Theatre in Pennsylvania, they invited me to do a one-night performance of *The Gospel According to Josh* for hundreds of their patrons in November, only a few months away. And just like that, my one-man show, living on borrowed time from this festival, had fresh blood running through its veins.

All of the writing and performing success I was having helped me feel slightly better than I had in a very long time yet surprisingly, only while my mind was occupied with work. Nights or solitary moments alone were a reminder of all of life's question marks—my sanity, my family, my dead father's regular visits, the girlfriend who wished she was a wife, and the career. Where was it all going and at what point would I get rid of the empty feeling inside? The thought of it all was too much to bear. I had to find a way to take on more work. This camel, susceptible to disability because of his weak back and knobby knees, and already carrying a heavy load, would soon accept the carriage of one last piece of straw, which wouldn't just break him, it would nearly kill him.

TWENTY-SEVEN

....

THE ONE-MAN (SIDE) SHOW

One evening following a performance of my one-man show, a young woman named Namakula approached me and asked, "What was it like doing a performance about your dead father?" Nobody had asked me that question before. The snarky part of my brain wanted to tell her that sometimes it was like living in a minimum-security prison and putting on a play about the cruel warden to audition for my early parole.

Instead I said, "It's certainly a challenge. To relive those memories—in the moment it feels like salt in the wound, but when it's all over it's pretty cathartic." That answer was also true. Take that snarky brain.

Namakula went on to explain that she had asked me about my father because she, too, had lost hers only a few weeks prior. From that initial conversation, Namakula and I became fast friends and a sounding board for one other in coping with the recent death of our respective patriarchs. I wasn't as open about my feelings other than what I divulged on stage, but Namakula's emotion was very raw and I found some comfort knowing that my words were able to lift her spirits in some way.

Namakula also happened to be a freelance artist, producing and starring in her very own Internet sitcom *Kate and Kula,* a dark comedy about the misadventures of two irreverent twenty-something professional women living in New York City. Filming began in August and she asked me to appear in an episode where the two title characters were negotiating a business deal with a potential client inside of a strip club.

I was to play the role of a disgruntled and oversexed Chuck E. Cheese store manager who frequented the strip club to de-stress from a hard day of dealing with horrible children, obnoxious parents, and the repetitious yammering of an oversized animatronic mouse.

Now that remedial college algebra was over (I passed) and the summer run of my one-man show was finished, I had a good deal of time on my hands. Taking this acting role was the perfect kind of work to occupy my mind and prevent the devil from using my newly idle hands as his workshop. This sitcom was no pressure, completely silly, and a lot of fun. But there was one little problem. Lara would not be happy knowing that I was participating in a project that featured overt and ostentatious displays of sexuality.

(—*Don't tell her. Keep your pinche mouth shut, ese.*—)

(—*Homie, ain't no way she gonna find out about this.*—)

(—*A fool who keeps silent is considered wise.*—)

A few years back, I had been cast in a play that required me to kiss another man on stage. Lara, ever the sweet and supportive girlfriend, traveled from New York City to Philadelphia to see my performance but ran out immediately after the show, sick to her stomach at what she had just witnessed.

"I had to watch you kiss another person." She was furious and her cheeks were flushed from a mélange of vomiting and crying.

"I'm sorry but it's just a part of my job. It doesn't mean anything," I assured her with a hint of nonchalance. I didn't see what the big deal was. I wasn't gay and I loved her. End of story.

"How would you feel if I started making out with someone in my office because it was 'part of my job'?"

Um, that would depend on whether that someone was your hot, young female secretary. Shut up snarky brain. I had no answer for her.

A few months prior to the festival run of my one-man show I fulfilled my actor obligations to Phil's theatre company. The role I had to play required I take part in a scene where I had to dry hump a prostitute on stage. When Lara found out, she threatened to break up with me unless I pantomimed for her in our bedroom the moves I had to make with the actress playing the prostitute. I reluctantly obliged.

Following Lara's attendance of the play, my reenactment in our bedroom was deemed wholly inaccurate and I was given a punishment far worse than the termination of our relationship—a three-month dose of the cold shoulder.

THE WORST LAP DANCE IN HISTORY

Filming for the episode was scheduled on a weekday on the Lower East Side in the basement lounge of a bar, which was remodeled and redressed to look like an actual strip club. What Lara didn't know wouldn't hurt her.

The first thing I noticed when I walked onto set was all of the half-naked women in the room with pasties on their boobs. The second thing I noticed was all of the men in the room pretending like they weren't staring at the half-naked women in the room with pasties on their boobs.

When it was time to film my scene, I was given fifteen different takes to improvise a few lines of dialogue while an actress, playing the part of a stripper, gave me the most uninspiring series of lap dances in the long history of lap dances.

For the record I've never actually received a lap dance, but from what I've read in *Cosmopolitan*—the magazine where I, along with millions of teenage American girls go for their sex advice—the dancer is supposed to grind their rear end in the region of their customer's genitals. However, all I got from this young lady was a little breeze across my kneecaps from the motion of her buttocks gyrating in my general direction.

A DIAMOND-STUDDED PAYOFF

A few weeks passed, and in between my full-time job and my preparation for *The Gospel According to Josh* at The Media Theatre production in November, I also had to plan something for my six-year anniversary with Lara on September 1st. Initially, I had thought about doing the safe and very typical flower and fancy restaurant thing. But something in my gut was telling me I had to make this anniversary special and do something epic; something to make up for my sin of omission in not telling her about my strip club scene; something to make up for avoiding her mere presence for more than six months; something that said, "I love you," which was true, in spite of my recent behavior; something that would throw her off the trail of my reluctance to hear wedding bells, yet something that would prevent me from losing another important person in my life. The only logical thing to do? I would actually ask her to marry me and have her twist my arm into setting a date later on. I think I had seen an episode of Seinfeld where

George did something very similar and it worked for him.

For a few days in late August, I spent much of my free time searching the web for any information I could find on diamond engagement rings—cultivating a fundamental knowledge of the complex world of cuts, carats, and color clarity.

During the late afternoon on the eve of our anniversary, I spotted the perfect ring while wandering through the Diamond District in midtown Manhattan. It was a simple yet elegant one-carat oval cut diamond with a platinum band.

Following a little price negotiation and a long talk about life and marriage with an eager young salesman newly married himself, I opened my wallet to pay for the ring but found my debit card—my only form of plastic payment—was missing.

"This is completely out of character for me. I'm so sorry. Can you please hold the ring until tomorrow? I'll either have a new card or cash for you then," I said, embarrassed at my careless oversight. This salesman, now more skeptical than eager, could have easily made two or three sales in the time we spent talking.

While considering my proposal he twirled the bottom of his wispy beard that barely covered his face. "For you—I will do this. The woman. She seems very important to you. Now go. Come back in the morning."

Instead of going through a long and drawn out process of calling my bank and having them forward me a replacement card, I went home first to see if I dropped or misplaced it somewhere inside my apartment. As I walked in the door, I dug through the left pocket of the cargo shorts I was wearing to remove my wallet. My hand hit the bottom of the pocket and a few square and plastic objects brushed against my knuckles. It was my debit card, an old student ID, and a supermarket rewards card—all of which must have slid out of their usual compartment in my wallet while I was walking around that afternoon. Crisis averted.

Another One Bites the Dust

That evening, Lara and I were both hanging out in the living room slash bedroom of our shoebox-sized apartment. I sat on the love seat in front of the television rehearsing my big proposal speech in my head while Lara sat ten feet away in her desk chair surfing the web.

(—*Papito, you're not getting sweaty and nervous over this girl?*—)

(—I don't know if she'll even say yes.—)

(—*The debit card thing must've been a sign, homes. Don't do this.*—)

(—I should go for a walk outside.—)

No sooner did I get up to put on a shirt did Lara spin around in her desk with her laptop in hand.

"What the hell is this?" she asked. She was livid. Her face was pink and ready to explode at any minute. She was pointing to the newsfeed in her Facebook profile. It was a picture of me getting what looked like a passionate lap dance during my scene in Namakula's web sitcom.

"Oh, it's just a webisode—a comedy. I did it a few weeks ago. I was super busy and I forgot to tell you. It totally slipped my mind."

"You pulled the same crap with that prostitute in your play in February. Why can't you just talk to me about this stuff?"

"It was not even originally in the script," I said. Though it was technically the truth, the picture of me with the stripper trumped that and was worth more than the customary thousand words. Lara only needed one.

"Bullshit."

"She's not even really giving me a lap dance."

"It looks real to me and it's embarrassing.

"It's an easy fix."

"I need to get away from you," she said, storming down the hallway bringing her laptop with her, slamming the bathroom door behind her.

While waiting for Lara to emerge from the bathroom, and with a beer in my hand, I did a little Facebook damage control by deleting the picture of me with the stripper. If I got rid of the evidence, we would have nothing to argue about and she couldn't stay mad at me. Within minutes I got an update that Lara had changed her status from "In a Relationship" to "Single."

I downed three beers within an hour, hoping that the alcohol would take the edge off of this stressful situation. It didn't. Another hour passed and she finally emerged from the bathroom fully dressed. Every floorboard creaked under her feet, like wooden piano keys as she made her way down the hallway to stand in front of me.

"How are you?" I asked while keeping my eyes fixed to the ground.

"Not good." Her monotone was perfectly pitched to match mine.

"Did you, um... did you change your relationship status to single?"

"I did."

"Well you're not serious, are you?" I asked finally looking away from the floor and directly into her eyes. They were bloodshot and her porcelain cheeks puffy and irritated from what I presumed to be tears.

"I am, Josh. I am serious. I can't trust you."

"Yes you can—"

"You don't want to be with me. You don't care how I feel and you haven't even tried to apologize."

"I'm sorry."

"It's a little late for that. I'm done with you, Josh."

"No. But our anniversary—"

"I have to do this. I'm going to stay with a friend tonight. I'm not sure when I'll see you next," she said, exiting our apartment with only a small purse in hand.

(—*Ditched three times in two years. Bitch, you got the plague.*—)

(—I deserved this one.—)

(—*And from your parents too, puto. No tienes nada. You're better off dead.*—)

(—I should fight for her. But I'm tired. When's it gonna get easier?—)

(—*O death, where is your victory?*—)

That night I fell asleep on my couch with two empty bottles of wine that served as my bedmates in the absence of my girlfriend. While in my slumber, I found myself alone in a familiar rainforest.

TWENTY-EIGHT

....

THE BLAME GAME

All of the vegetation—the treetops, the flowers, and even the tall grass—had drooped over and wilted to the ground. The face of Ghost Dad eclipsed the sun and blocked out all natural light.

"What are you going to do?" he asked.

"What do you care? This is all your fault. I'm turning into you."

"You make your own decisions—"

"Stop bothering me. Just let me go," I said, cutting him off.

"You're not going anywhere. It's time to wake."

JOSH RIVEDAL

TWENTY-NINE

....

REASONS WHY NOT TO PUT A BAND-AID OVER A SEVERED LIMB

A whole two weeks passed and Lara didn't come home and wouldn't return my phone calls or texts. Meanwhile I continued to spend a great deal of time in preparation for my one-night engagement of *The Gospel According to Josh* at The Media Theatre in early November—an opportunity that needed to go off without a hitch to appease the pestering ghost.

When not rehearsing and rewriting, my days were occupied with calculus and public speaking classes at Baruch College in addition to my full-time restaurant job. Free nights were spent in my hermitage of an apartment getting blitzed on an assortment of pale ale and red wine while sitting in front of the television watching *The Princess Bride* and *Law & Order: SVU* reruns. Anything I could do to distract myself from my guilt and sadness over Lara.

Into late September and through the first week of October I saw her a grand total of three times. The first time was when she accompanied me to the Midtown International Theatre Festival awards ceremony. I was nominated for "Best Performance in a Solo Show" and practically begged her over the phone to be my date. I dare say that I was a shoo-in for the award and figured that a win would remind her of the good parts from our past, showing her that I was actually a somebody—a person worthy of a second chance. This award was as close to owning a mansion in West Egg as I could get, and she my Daisy Buchanan.

All I could think about was winning that award so I could tell Lara how sorry I was for hurting her. I played the scene in my head over and over. I'd walk up to the podium and accept my trophy, or whatever they were giving away. I'd make a poignant and hilarious acceptance speech, take Lara outside, look her in the eyes, and apologize to her. She'd accept and then in slow motion, I'd take her in my arms and give her one of those legendary once-in-a-lifetime kisses straight out of the movies—like that passionate Rachel McAdams and Ryan Gosling kiss in the middle of a rainstorm from *The Notebook.*

Lara avoided me until the day of the ceremony and met me outside of the event hall, a large theater in midtown. We made very little eye contact and shared an awkward hug. "You look... you look pretty," I said. She looked like an exquisite, slightly wilted flower, beautiful but fatigued. I hoped my compliment would perk her up, if only for a moment.

She gave me a once-over, the penitent man donned in khakis, tan-and-ivory-colored loafers with no socks, and a red and white striped fitted dress shirt with a white collar.

"You look good," she said with a smile, "like a handsome, gay candy cane." Touché. The silently remorseful gay candy cane could only laugh that one off. He had it coming. The awards ceremony was a short one and my category wasn't until the end. My transcendental plan for wooing Lara backfired when I didn't win "Best Performance" in the categories of "Solo Show" or in "Trying to Look Cool While Losing." The night got worse when we went to dinner at a Japanese fusion restaurant to bury the hatchet. Our small talk was labored if not painful. Somewhere in my Neanderthaloid mind, I deduced that flirting with the waitress would make me look desirable to my venerable Mrs. Buchanan. But my shenanigans did nothing except make me look like a jackass, and I left the restaurant alone that night.

The next time I saw Lara was more than a week later when she came by to pick up some extra clothes. Though she was aiming to avoid me because she thought I'd be out, our conversation was a little more fluid and enjoyable. She ended up spending the night lying beside me in our bed but left the following morning without notice. The mixed signals she was sending were dizzying.

She didn't speak to me again until the following week when she came over to tell me she wasn't renewing the lease on our apartment, which was expiring on November 30th.

Time Is Up

It was the second to last Sunday in October and I was laying in my bed wide awake at 7 a.m. only having slept a few hours, as a result of a visit from my dead father for the third day in a row. Rays of sunlight gradually poked their way through the cracks between the giant window next to my bed and the curtains that hung unevenly over its face.

I had to work a brunch shift at my restaurant job in a few hours and was physically exhausted from working a twelve-hour double shift the day prior. But since I couldn't sleep, I wanted to do something productive so I rolled out of bed, showered, ate a little breakfast, and started in on some calculus homework.

At around 9 a.m., my brain needed a little break from binomials and derivatives so I surfed around ESPN.com for a bit and then checked my email where there was a new message from Lara, who I hadn't heard from in a few weeks.

Hey Josh

Though September was emotionally charged and extremely draining, the challenges of those weeks have faded into something very unexpected. I have started dating someone. I am taking things very slowly, but I wanted to tell you everything up front. This is not easy for me to admit because I care about you very deeply, but I wanted to tell you straight out because you are important to me and the time that we shared over the past six years makes it critical for me to be honest with you. He is a very nice guy and I think I am starting to really care about him, which let me know it was time to tell you. I am very sorry if this hurts you. That is the last thing I want to do, but not telling you feels like lying and I didn't want to do that either. I care for you a great deal Josh.

Love always,
Lara

(—After six weeks? I thought I'd have more time...—)
(—*Say word? You said that about your father.*—)
(—That wasn't my fault.—)
(—*Y tu mama tambien? That wasn't your fault either, right?*—)
(—*To everything there is a season. A time to be born, a time to die...*—)
(—No. Stop it! I can't. I'm not my father.—)

I had to vacate that apartment as soon as humanly possible. With a little more than a month left on the lease and two weeks till the production in Media, I couldn't bear to live in a place whose walls absorbed our collective joys, our arguments, and our occasional moans of ecstasy. I wanted nothing more than to forget this woman—but more so, I wanted to forget that the past eighteen months of my life existed. I couldn't do that yet. Not entirely. I hadn't been released from the bonds of Ghost Dad.

I immediately put out a message on Facebook and through all of my email lists that I was looking to move somewhere within the five boroughs of New York City, any time within the next seven days, and would do anything and pay anything to have them help me find an empty room to stay in.

Two days later I got an email message from a woman named Karen, a friend of a friend on the Broadway national tour of *Hair*, who had a room available the first week of November. She wanted us to meet in person later in the week at her apartment in Harlem to make sure I was suitable roommate material. Even if I had to sleep on the floor with a dozen stray cats, I would find a way to move in with Karen and get on with what little life I had left.

140TH AND BROADWAY

Saturday that same week, I made the forty-five-minute bus and train ride uptown to meet with Karen. I got to her neighborhood an hour early to see what kind of people were living there, the amenities it had to offer, and whether I had to carry a concealed weapon while walking the streets.

It was a demographic much different from my current neighborhood on the Upper East Side inhabited by a large number of Jewish families, professional athletes, young artists, and rich old women with mangled faces due to some back-alley plastic surgery.

Unlike most neighborhoods below 140th street, this one didn't have much to offer in the way of good restaurants unless you counted the Burger King, McDonalds, and the place that served *mofongo* a few blocks down on Broadway.

There were barbershops on every block, all filled with young Latino men, some with their children getting their hair cut and others sitting around chatting or watching whatever soccer match was playing on TV. There was a single shabby-looking grocery store filled to the brim with wilted produce and cans of Goya beans stacked at least fifty feet high like a pyramid that nearly reached the ceiling—one of the lesser-known Wonders of the World.

It was an abnormally warm day for November in New York City. Small crowds of people were gathered outside huddled near every stoop, bench, and lamppost. Old and young men alike were sitting around card tables playing dominoes on the sidewalks while women and men of all ages were watching them play or scratching off lottery tickets.

I was born into a neighborhood very similar to this one and if I had to guess, most of the people there were surviving under or near the poverty line just like my own family once had. On the bright side, these people seemed happy and even friendly and if I moved in with Karen I could practice my mediocre Spanish with the chatty *abuelitas* sitting in their lawn chairs on the street corner.

I was on time for my meet-and-greet with Karen and arrived at a six-story brick building in need of repair. It must have housed hundreds of tenants and was demoralizing just to look at it. I rang the buzzer that had Karen's name attached and within a few seconds the building made a funny humming sound and invited me to enter.

After climbing four flights of stairs, littered with cigarette butts and beer bottle caps, I was greeted at the front door by a gorgeous mixed race woman probably in her late twenties.

"Hi. Are you Josh?" she asked, holding the door open just a crack.

"Yes, that's me."

"I'm Tanya, Karen's roommate. Come on in."

The inside of the apartment was much different than everything I had seen of the rest of that building. It was actually clean and smelled of lilacs. The window ledges were ornamented with a few tiny houseplants, and the walls decorated in fresh paint and a few pieces of Central African artwork.

Karen, an athletic young woman probably in her mid-twenties who looked as if her ancestors hailed from the shores of Caucasia, soon emerged from her bedroom. We shared a smile, a warm handshake, and two "hellos," then the two ladies gave me a grand tour of the apartment. The kitchen and bathroom were both neat and modestly decorated with a feminine touch. My soon-to-be bedroom was a large room in the back of the apartment, not littered with stray cats but office supplies waiting to be hauled off and put into storage.

Finally, the three of us congregated in the living room for polite banter and discussion of the potential living arrangements.

(—*Yo papi, I got dibs on Tanya...*—)

(—*You idiots need to behave. That is not happening.*—)

In fact, it was out of the question. I would be sharing the apartment with Karen and Tanya's husband, Eric, for the next six months. Tanya was leaving to go on tour. In less than fifteen minutes, I was escorted out of the apartment. "We will put our heads together and have an answer for you tomorrow," said Karen and Tanya in perfect harmony.

THE BATH SLIPPERS' LAST HURRAH

The next day, Sunday, was the beginning of my hump week. Wednesday was my big performance at The Media Theatre, an offering to Ghost Dad that I hoped would be deemed worthy. And if given the green light, I would move in with Karen and Tanya on Thursday.

That morning I worked a brunch shift slinging eggs and seafood and then returned to my apartment to put a few of my worldly possessions into boxes. Karen finally called late into the evening to tell me they liked my company and I could move in whenever I was ready. Great news. I would call a moving company in the morning.

Monday was one big long cram session. I rehearsed the script and tweaked my writing the entire day. No time for liquor, Facebook, or sorrowful introspection over the girl and the home I was forced to leave behind. Oh, and the movers were set to come on Thursday evening.

Tuesday was spent packing my life into boxes—clothes, Haakon's American flag, my father's diary that sent me to Vancouver, and trophies I received as a child from my church for reciting thousands of Bible verses. There was a square, plastic, miniature briefcase that contained my old clarinet and all the reeds I had purchased back in the fifth grade. This one was coming with me in case I ever wanted to make money playing "Hot Cross Buns" and "Mary had a Little Lamb" at weddings and *quinceañeras*. There was one shoebox that had some family photos and a couple of old love letters sent to and from Lara—a reminder about the beginnings of our relationship, nostalgia which, for a few moments, soothed the throbbing pain of a wounded soul.

Just then, my pants pocket began to vibrate and the reminiscent spell of which I was under had been broken. It was a text message from Lara. She was coming by the apartment on Thursday to make sure I didn't take any of her stuff. The sentiment I felt for her quickly melted into anger for the seamless and carefree transition to another man—easily discarded like I was some pair of moldy old bathslippers or moth-eaten underwear. So, I took the collection of those love letters and pictures and shoved them into the paper shredder one by one until the physical evidence of our love was gone and all that was left were pieces of confetti for a future pity party.

THIRTY

....

A HUMP DAY VISIT

Wednesday was the big day of the big show. I rode three different trains through New York, New Jersey, and Pennsylvania to get to The Media Theatre.

This was one of the most important days of my life. My former colleagues (and my father, it would seem) were putting an enormous amount of trust in me to present this new creation of mine to their friends, acquaintances, employees, and benefactors. I felt a tremendous obligation and responsibility to make them proud, delivering a good show as promised. And my gut (who had become very talkative lately) was telling me if I blew this performance out of the water then they might ask me to come back to do the show again for a longer run with a larger audience—which was probably exactly what Ghost

Dad wanted. He visited me after I dozed off a few minutes into my second train ride.

THIRTY-ONE

STAY THE COURSE

I was lying on my back in the middle of the rain-forest looking up at the night sky. A feeling of complete and utter peace flowed through my body—a sensation that was peculiar but exhilarating. Within a few moments the stars swirled together in the patterns of a hyperactive kaleidoscope, until they formed a small orb of light that was shooting straight toward me. A heavy rain began to fall and soaked every inch of my body. An aggressive wind lifted me up till I was floating upright a few hundred feet off the ground. Paunchy raindrops bounced off my face as the orb of light came closer, forming a face with which I had become rather familiar.

"You're becoming distracted," Ghost Dad said with a disapproving glare.

"I'm still in love with her... Lara—"

"Today's work is paramount. Focus."

"I'm just tired," I said, defensive at his scornful tone. "I don't think I can do this for you anymore."

"Stay the course. This has always been as much for you as it has been for me."

And with that, his face and the orb of light dissipated into the night sky as millions of tiny stars.

The rain was now pouring down faster, pelting me in the face, and the blustery wind that had lifted me off the ground had come to a complete halt. My body flipped around and shot toward the ground like a bullet, face first. Just before my nose grazed a single blade of grass, I woke and it was time to switch to the third and final train that would take me to the theater.

THIRTY-TWO

....

A HAIL MARY AND A
PROPOSAL

I spent that last leg of my trip to Media trying to figure out why the ghost of my dead father had been pushing me and haunting me as if he was doing me some sort of favor. Was it like the times as a child when I received excessive beatings to correct my behavior because "it was for my own good"?

Despite the protest I offered in my dream, there were parts of doing this one-man show that I absolutely enjoyed, namely performing. But I had to wonder whether Ghost Dad's pet project was worth the sleeplessness crippling my brain and the hundreds of hours of time that I would never get back? For the time being, it was. Whatever this dead man's motive, it intrigued me just enough to want to try to figure out how to continue on with this project after my one-night performance at The Media Theatre.

Once I arrived at the theater, an ornate former vaudeville house, I found my old friends on the administrative staff hard at work, planning for the next show in their season. I shook hands, gave hugs, and may have even kissed a few babies to practice for the potential politicking I'd have to do on behalf of my show later that night.

Ten minutes before show time and I was fully stretched and ready to give the performance of a lifetime. Looking out across the stage and into the seats, expecting to see a full house, I found only one person sitting in the audience. It was the theater's technical director, Grizzly, a burly, bearded man in his early thirties who was running my lights and sound.

(—How am I supposed to get invited back like this?—)

(—*You're a human Pepe LePew. That stink follows you everywhere, dawg.*—)

(—This has to work. I have no other options.—)

(—*You need a miracle, puto. Divine intervention. A...*—)

(—*...Hail Mary, full of grace...*—)

Ironically, the five words of the Hail Mary that I could recall after watching *The Godfather II* earlier in the week brought in five new audience members. With only a minute to spare, Grizzly waved me over to the side of the stage for a private powwow.

(—*No mames, hijo. He's gonna pull the show. Not enough people.*—)

(—Oh, God... that's the look of pity on his face.—)

"Hey, man," he whispered. "Hang tight. We're holding for another five minutes or so. We have to wait for a couple of the theater's board members. They're running late."

"Cool," was the only word with which I could think to respond.

Relief.

(—*Something, something, blessed art thou amongst women and blessed...*—)

(—*...is the fruit of thy womb, Jesus.*—)

(—*Holy Mary! We just got like twenty-five more people. It's an audience...*—)

(—*Nah, dawg, it's a drum circle.*—)

(—It's better than nothing. I'll take it.—)

The theatre's artistic director, Jesse, got up on stage to say a few words.

"Some of you may already know the young man I'm about to introduce—Josh Rivedal, a dear friend and frequent collaborator. We worked together on a little piece called *Thrill Me* a few years back and he was fantastic in it. I'm so proud of him for putting together his own cabaret which you're about to see."

(—*Oh hell, no. This ain't no cabaret. This is some serious ass theatre...*—)

(—*Dude, I know. I know. Just relax. We'll show 'em.*—)

The lights went completely black and the sound of applause from sixty hands brought the lights on stage back up. There I sat on a tall wooden stool playing that overzealous Sunday school teacher once again.

From the very top of the show, I could feel those thirty souls in front of me breathing along with me, our collective hearts beating as one. At my best lines, one middle-aged black man with a neat box-fade haircut and charming smile would let out a squealing and infectious laugh that encouraged the rest of the audience to join in his amusement. At one point I looked over to find a twelve-year-old boy and his mother firmly planted in their seats, holding each other, and totally engrossed in everything I was saying. I had never had anyone under the age of twenty in the audience before. And the sight of this mother-son combo was an added bonus, a picture of what could have been and a flicker of hope for what still might exist with my own mother.

Before I knew it the seventy-five-minute show was over. Stage lights were fading to black and then rose again to illuminate both me and the audience. I was being hailed with light applause as a few ebullient youngsters in the back stood to their feet.

Having already exited the stage, I was brought back out by Jesse for an impromptu question and answer session with the audience.

"How did you find the inspiration to write this show?" one young writer asked.

I danced around that question with the ease of a one-legged ballerina but made no mention of Vancouver or Ghost Dad.

"Are you still bitter about your father and what he did to you?" asked a gray-haired, heavy-set, middle-aged woman.

"It depends on the day, I guess. It's a bit more complicated than just 'bitter,'" I replied with a certain defusing coyness. I didn't want to take up their entire evening with a dissertation on my true feelings about the man.

"What kinds of movies do you like?" asked an unusual older man wearing Harry Potter-style glasses.

"Low-brow comedies and anything that I'm in," I answered with a wink.

"What plans do you have in show business and life?" asked the middle-aged black man with the squealing laugh.

"A three-hour train ride home and some sleep," I quipped.

As everyone filed out, I began to gather my belongings. Jesse flagged me down from his seat and asked, "Could we could talk about a few things?"

(—*Don't get crazy, bizcocho. They only do musicals here.*—)

(—*It ain't happening, dawg. He ain't asking you back.*—)

(—Shit. I know. I know.—)

"Sit down, Joshua," said Jesse. "That was wonderful. The audience loved it. A board member of the theater was here and loved it as well."

"Thank you," I said politely as I felt my face contorting into a sheepish grin.

"We would love to have *The Gospel According to Josh* back at The Media Theatre next year as part of our season—"

"That would be great," I said, cutting him off in great earnest.

"You'd have to reformat it a little. It needs to include more songs and musical theatre references. Would you be interested in something like that?"

Was I interested? That depended. Was I interested in becoming a professionally produced playwright? Was I interested in performing a show at a place where Broadway actors performed? Was I interested in having this theater that usually played it safe with *The Sound of Music* and *Titanic* take a risk on my unknown show? Was I interested in getting Ghost Dad off my back? I'd have to think about it for a few days.

"Yes, yes, of course," I answered immediately with a poker face that belied my internal celebrating.

"Excellent, Joshua. We will continue this dialogue over the next few months," he said as we shook hands followed by a bear hug.

I thanked the rest of the theater's staff and hustled my way out the door. Fifty yards away from the theater in the middle of the street, I let out a loud cry, a yell of relief and thanks that the garbage from the last eighteen months was turning into solid gold. That three-hour trip back to New York was spent with my rear end stuck to the seat and my head in the clouds.

A "No" Forever

Thursday morning, excitement over my one-man show was tempered with the realization that I'd have to spend my day working toward vacating a place I called home with a woman who wanted to have nothing to do with me.

The doorbell rang and it was Lara. I unlocked the padlock and opened the front door where she stood staring at the floor, refusing to look at me.

"Hi," I said.

"Hi," she said back.

"I'm keeping the air-conditioner."

"Fine."

"Why don't you come in?" I asked.

"Thanks."

"How have you been?" I asked as she made her way to a corner of the apartment far away from me to refold clothes she'd left behind, already in perfectly symmetrical squares.

"Fine," she said

"How is your living situation right now?"

"Fine," she answered without looking up from her busywork.

It occurred to me right then and there that I still had one shot left at winning her back.

"Listen, I have something I want to ask you."

(—*Oh, Lord, do not do this, homeboy. You don't even have a ring.*—)

(—*It is better to live in a desert land than with a quarrelsome and fretful woman.*—)

(—But I don't want to be alone... and she isn't quarrelsome or fretful.—)

(—*He was talking about you, pendajo.*—)

"I've been thinking—well, maybe not, but I don't want to lose you. And I just, I should've asked you this a long time ago."

She looked up at me for the first time. Her body clenched up and her breath grew short. Her words were barely audible.

"This isn't the right time for that. I don't—"

"Just hear me out," I said, cutting her off. "I should've done this a long time ago and I'm an idiot for waiting so long. I want to know—will you marry me?"

Her eyes welled up with tears, her perfectly formed pink lips now turned downward.

"No, Josh. No. I can't. I'm with somebody else."

(—*Thou shalt not lust after thy neighbor's wife... or girlfriend.*—)

"But are you in love with him?"

"I'm with someone else."

(—*Don't do it, burro...*—)

"Will you marry me?" I asked while placing all of my body's weight down on one knee, now touching the floor, my joints and muscles deflating in preparation for the obvious disappointment of what was about to come next.

"Don't do that, Josh. No."

"Are you sure?"

"You didn't include me in your life—"

"I know and I was scared and I am sorry. I should have—"

"It's too late for that," she said, giving me the stop sign with one hand while wiping her tears with the other.

I couldn't do anything but turn around to hide my own tears, pretending to tidy up the apartment that was no longer my own.

My place in her heart was now occupied by another and there was nothing I could do to reclaim it. Never in my life had I experienced rejection without some glimmer of hope that someday I could change the outcome back in my favor. My mother had eventually come back to me for forgiveness and even my father had returned to manifest himself my dreams. But Lara's rejection of my marriage proposal was not a "no for now"; it was a "no forever."

MY HEART WILL (PROBABLY) GO ON

When the movers arrived, the two of us reached deep inside of ourselves to become partners in an old song and dance routine of smiling and playful chatting for an audience of strangers while secretly going through a long-term private disagreement.

Within ninety minutes the meager entirety of my worldly possessions were down five flights of stairs and placed inside a moving truck that could have fit three times the amount of what I had. I sent the movers on their way to my new 140th Street apartment with the chatty *abuelitas* and the all-night barbershops, and then came back upstairs to do a final sweep of my now former apartment.

With a once-over through closets and old dressers, there was nothing left I wanted or needed except the girl still standing by the window. When we hugged goodbye, her tiny arms felt much bigger than their actual size. It seemed as if they might swallow me up forever. I hadn't had physical contact with anyone since our anniversary slash breakup and it felt good to be touched, to have the slightest bit of warm human touch.

I let go of her with a kiss on the forehead and the promise that she'd always be a friend. I then hurried as fast as I could down five flights of stairs and into the street without looking back. Somehow life had to go on. I had to plow ahead with my head down, business as usual, much like the last eighteen months. And so I hailed a cab, jumped in, gave directions to my new apartment, and fought back tears while my chatty cab driver prattled on end-lessly about women, specifically his three wives back home in Africa and how they were all "a pain in my ass."

Later that evening I got a text message from my dear old mother.

- I LOVE YOU JOSH. I WONDER IF UR COMING DOWN 4 THANKSGIVING THIS YEAR. WE ALL WANT TO SEE YOU

With the move, the breakup, and the perfor-mance in Media, I completely forgot that my favor-ite holiday was just around the corner. This year I didn't care to celebrate much of anything unless it involved copious amounts of alcohol to help numb my brain. But our Thanksgiving tradition had al-ways been a teetotaler's dream. I could sit in my new apartment eating a microwavable turkey dinner with a few bottles of wine and the pugnacious voic-es in my head. But I could also go down to New Jersey and have creamed corn and canned cranberry sauce with my mother, the only parent I had suc-cessfully avoided for the better part of a year.

I still couldn't seem to forget my mother's be-trayal and any text message from her that started off with, "I love you," or "I'm thinking about you," made me a special kind of angry that brought out my inner, green Lou Ferrigno. JOSH SMASH!

However, I did want to see my brother and sister and the Kozlowski family with whom we'd shared holidays since I was a little boy. The idea of spending the holiday alone seemed downright pitiful, so I agreed to come down to visit for a few hours on Thanksgiving Day.

Thanksgiving morning I took an overcrowded train from Penn Station in Manhattan down to Hamilton, New Jersey where I was met by my mother and brother.

"Hi," I said, greeting them each with an unaffectionate one-armed hug.

A short, speechless five-minute drive brought us to the Kozlowski house. The patriarch of the family, a round-bellied balding Polish-America man, greeted me with a handshake-hug at the door and subsequently flipped me around onto the living room couch and hunched over me till a loud and pungent stream of noxious gas emitted from his rear end and into my face—a toxic clouded gift he hadn't bestowed upon me since my childhood. For some, that would have been terrifying and embarrassing but for me it was a brief moment of normalcy, something I hadn't felt in the eighteen months since my father died.

My sister and her new husband, Joe, arrived a few minutes after we did. One of the older Kozlowski children canceled at the last minute to stay home with a sick baby. A few usual non-family holiday guests canceled for one reason or another. And the eldest Kozlowski son canceled as well and for good reason. At his wife's parents' house they celebrated with alcohol and a bold, saucy Puerto Rican turkey. I would have done anything to spend the holiday with them and away from our sober celebration complete with lackluster Caucasian turkey.

The house was as empty as it had ever been for a holiday. Everyone was moving on with their lives and having babies and in-laws and Puerto Rican turkey while I was in the same place as I'd always been—another Thanksgiving living in New York, barely managing a mediocre career in show business while trying to put on a good face about it in front of everyone, except this year I was doing it all alone.

When the nine of us sat down to dinner, everyone (except my mother) wanted to talk about how much they missed my father or poke fun at some funny or strange thing he used to do.

"What was that ridiculous song he used to play on the piano? It was like the only song he knew."

"Remember how he always thanked God for the bounty when he prayed? Weird."

"I miss having him here."

"Me too."

I couldn't bring myself to join in on the fun, afraid I would hear about it from Ghost Dad later that night.

My silence brought questions from the peanut gallery who wanted to know what happened between Lara and me because "She was such a *nice* girl."

Generic answers like, "It just didn't work out," and "we just weren't meant to be together," made for bland side dishes to the Caucasian turkey. I secretly wished I could sneak away from the table and crawl into a dark pit somewhere to hide out from the world for a few months. In between dinner and dessert, I managed to sneak away to the upstairs bathroom for some alone time. A place where I could have an intimate conversation with the man looking back at me in the oversized vanity mirror.

(—*What's wrong, dawg? You had big plans after your dad died.*—)

(—Nothing I did changed anything.—)

(—*Cabrón, el mismo que su padre. You're no different than him.*—)

(—*You were made in his image.*—)

(—Why can't I just be normal?—)

(—*Yo, normal people don't think about drinking that bleach beside the toilet. Just do it.*—)

I raced down the stairs and back to the first floor where everyone was either watching football, eating cake, or passed out in a food coma. In front of the television, I ate as much as I could to distract myself from the mental refuse swirling around inside my head. Soon enough I passed out from an overdose of tryptophan. I woke an hour later to the loud snores of my brother who was lying on the other end of the beige L-shaped sectional couch.

The house had even fewer people than before. From the dining room came the hubbub of Mrs. Kozlowski, my mother, my sister, and my brother-in-law, arguing over a game of Trivial Pursuit. A little sleep along with the snorts of my brother, the noise of the football game, and the sounds of angry women and gloating men in the room next to me helped drown out the voices, who were planning to mount an evening comeback.

The ensuing weeks brought about several forgettable one-night stands with a few female friends. With each, I hoped to put an end to my heartache, but with each the pain grew worse. Christmas arrived in no time and was a near replica of Thanksgiving. Escaping to my fortress of solitude in the upstairs bathroom, unable to run from persistent thoughts of my ex-girlfriend, I text-messaged her with a MERRY X-MAS and the suggestion that we get together for a friendly drink sometime soon. You know, for old times' sake—the only reason to ever do anything with anyone who you've royally pissed off. She responded immediately that she would be open to meeting for dinner the first week of the New Year.

I couldn't believe she actually wanted to see me. I had something to look forward to and a reason to shave the unkempt beard on my face now creeping halfway down my neck.

Speaking of the New Year, my resolutions for 2011 were straightforward and simple. I gave myself a full year to figure out the current question marks in my life—the ex, the family, Ghost Dad, and some sort of method to tune out the fatalistic dialogue from the three-headed triumvirate of mercurial voices in my head who shared the traits of an astute philosopher and a rabid attack dog. This camel needed an industrial-sized back brace and two knee replacements, and fast.

THIRTY-THREE

MOVING ON

The first morning of 2011, I awoke at sunrise under a pile of maroon-colored sheets and one big, fat, black, down comforter. I rubbed the morning crusties out of my eyes and stretched out a bit while letting out a hearty yawn. Laying face up, I put my hands behind my head, pleased with myself for having survived the year 2010 in one piece.

In my head I recapped the previous year—giving my sister away at her wedding in place of my father, the frequent visitations from the ghost, my artistic growth in developing my one-man show, my breakup with Lara, the calamity with Phil and his theatre company, a return to college, and everything with my mother. If I could get through all that in one year, good and bad, then 2011 would be a piece of cake. Bad things happen in threes and I got mine out of the way—my father, my mother, and Lara.

My schedule during that first week of the New Year was much different from what I was used to and a bit of a curveball. College was on hiatus for a few more weeks, no acting work was available (January and July traditionally being the worst times of year for that kind of thing in case you're contemplating a career change) and there was nothing I needed to do with *The Gospel According to Josh*. I was so drained from those last few months of the year that I hadn't thought ahead about what I was going to do with myself between school semesters. I was so used to moving and working long hours at a furious pace that the prospect of having nothing to do wasn't some sort of vacation or a blessing—it was the fifth layer of boredom hell. I tried to fill my time during that first week by calling up old friends I'd lost touch with, but all of them were too busy or too disinterested to resume our friendship.

For Old Time's Sake

On the eve of our supposed platonic tryst, New York City got blanketed with a few inches of snow. I was pleased to find that Lara didn't cancel due to the inclement weather. I arrived a few minutes early and waited outside on the sidewalk covered in salt crystals and mounds of partially melted, muddy snow. She arrived fashionably late at ten past the hour.

"You look good," I said as we took our seats. And she did despite looking tired and much thinner than the last time I saw her.

"No, I've been sick for a few days," she answered abruptly, not comfortable with the compliment I paid her.

"Well thank you for not canceling on me."

The next five minutes or so was filled with an uncomfortable stream of inconsequential chitchat about current events and the weather, finally interrupted by the waitress who wanted to take our order.

(—*Do it! Tell her you love her, papi. Eres mi canela, mi ciela...*—)

(—I'm not telling her she's my cinnamon *or* my sky, you psychopath.—)

"How were your holidays?" she asked.

I locked eyes with my dinner companion. "Some of the best I can remember." A boldfaced lie intended to show her I was doing fine without her.

"How were yours?" I asked. She replied in great detail about spending time with her family. Hearing about them brought about a sharp pain in my stomach because I loved and missed them dearly. I considered them an extension of my own family. Her father was a Marine and a straight shooter who treated me like I was his son. Her mother was someone I saw as near perfect—helpful, understanding, kind, nurturing but not overly so, and comfortable settling disputes outside of a courtroom. I wasn't too close with her sister but she was always sweet to me. Her niece and nephew, six and two years old, were little redheaded sweethearts with whom I read bedtime stories, changed diapers, kissed boo-boos, and played any number of games we invented together. I lost two families in the last eighteen months.

Finishing up at the restaurant and while parting ways, she whispered into my ear, "It was great to see you," and lovingly wrapped her arms around me the way she did the day I moved out of our apartment.

She went one way, presumably to head home, while I went for a little walk uptown trudging through the snow. I needed some space to think.

(—Homeboy, it ain't gonna happen. Get off of it.—)

(—You remember the ending to your parents little parable, don't you?—)

(—I don't have to end up like him.—)

(—Quizás pero, you're a lot more like your father than you think.—)

(—Stop saying that. Only in name and protruding forehead.—)

A few minutes into my introspective stroll, I got a text message from Lara.

- HEY, I DON'T KNOW IF WE SHOULD KEEP SEEING EACH OTHER LIKE THIS. IT'S NOT FAIR TO MY BOYFRIEND. BUT WE CAN DEFINITELY EMAIL AND TEXT MESSAGE. SORRY. :s

(—He was despised and rejected...—)

(—Shot down again, beeyotch.—)

(—You know what you need? You need to get drunk, borracho. Shit-faced.—)

(—Not by myself. I should call somebody... I should call Doc.—)

Is a Doc-tor in the House?

Meridoc, or Doc, was an old friend. He was a few years older than me, a true Jersey boy, the son of former hippies (they named him after a character in *The Lord of the Rings*), and a total free spirit. Somewhat of a beefcake type, Doc wore tank tops in the dead of winter, could down three beers before you finished your first, and had an assortment of odd jobs that included house painter, bartender, amateur neighborhood lawn specialist, and musical theatre actor. We met during the summer of 2004, cast as two of the four male leads in a workshop production of an untitled doo-wop themed musical theatre show ambitiously aiming for Broadway. Doc and I became fast friends after discovering that we shared the deep connection of having both hooked up with same actress in the cast, though not at the same time—an ordeal from which I thankfully emerged canker-free.

I rarely saw Doc after that bittersweet summer and it had been more than a year since he and I had spoken. Now that I was single and a bit brokenhearted, I needed a friend with which to commiserate and share a pint.

Doc wasn't available that night but we made plans for later in the week. He invited me to a screening party for an episode of the television show *Millionaire Love Match* that was taking place inside a swanky Manhattan hotel.

The night of the party, Doc and I met up at a bar near the hotel. He explained that he had gotten himself on this particular episode of *Millionaire Love Match* as a contestant, "looking for love." Though after meeting his millionaire love match later in the night I was pretty sure he did the show for the television exposure. She was rude, unfriendly, and sloppily overweight. Not only was she not Doc's type, she probably wasn't anyone else's either. Her shallow soul was seemingly made up of an abhorrent amalgamation of deep-seated anger, over-priced designer dresses, and slow roasted baby back ribs.

Doc and I got separated rather quickly. Throughout the night I found myself by the bar drinking anything and everything put in front of me. I smoked my way through two packs of cigarettes, and made out with any single, inebriated woman in sight. I was a miserable, stumbling, and fermented cloud of Marlboros, Red Bull, and vodka.

Thankfully I left the hotel that night alive and with no bumps, bruises, or STDs. I arrived back at my apartment safe and sound at the ripe hour of three a.m. Just before falling asleep and still in my drunken haze, I had little chat with myself, a release of the toxic vapors condensing inside my head. "You're an idiot. You don't want to live like this, partying and bnflgh, making out with fghho strange women. You're better than this, Jogpsjk. You're better than gftfat. You mother-fnhjbder. You miss Larhghhga. You're better thabjhu..."

That very night I was paid another visit from Ghost Dad, the first time in a fortnight that I had seen him.

THIRTY-FOUR

DO AS I SAY, NOT AS I DO

I was standing in a rainforest as usual, at the edge of a ravine. It was nighttime, but there was no moon or stars, just a single orb of light in the sky that was now shooting straight toward me. It stopped a few yards away from me. The orb floated over the ravine and morphed itself into the perfect dream-state version of my father, The Adonis Viking himself. His eyes held the weight of a deep sadness, the kind I saw in him in the months just before his suicide.

"You're unhappy." He spoke as if it was a matter-of-fact, but with a sense of empathy and compassion he had never given me before.

"I miss her. I don't have anyone—"

"That is a choice," he scolded, cutting me short before I could finish my thought.

"What about the choice you made?" I asked out of curiosity and anger.

"That is my cross to bear. This one is yours. And you will soon have another choice to make. Don't make the same—"

"What choice will I have to make?"

"It's time to wake, son."

THIRTY-FIVE

....

A NEAR-DEATH EXPERIENCE

That morning I woke early to go to work and was greeted with an evil hangover and a mouth that tasted like lipstick and cigarette butts. But there was something inside my body that felt much worse than the severe headache pounding like two jackhammers at the backs of my eye sockets. My stomach was twisted in knots and my soul, my entire being, felt as if it was drowning at sea while being drenched in hot flames. My tongue, my brain, my fingernails, my hair, my earlobes, my teeth, and the wrinkles at the seams of each arm and leg were all throbbing in pain.

I gingerly rolled out of bed to start my day but lost control of my limbs and collapsed on the hardwood floor. Tears poured from my eyes harder and faster than ever before and I couldn't make them stop. My mind was overrun only with thoughts of my stupid behavior the night prior, Lara, and how I hated myself for missing her. Lacking a mother, a father, and a surplus of friends I felt completely and entirely alone, sequestered on the dank, gloomy island of Loserville.

School was closed for another few weeks and *The Gospel According to Josh* was on hiatus. I had no busywork other than my soul-sucking restaurant job to distract me from the awareness of my physical and emotional solitude.

(—How did everything turn to shit so fast?—)

(—*Ese... it was show business. Eso mierda took over your life.*—)

(—My ambition. It was all-encompassing. It ruined everything.—)

(—*Are you to continue in this sin, this gluttony of self?*—)

(—No. I have to quit the business.—)

(—*You're worthless piece of shit, dawg. You have to quit everything.*—)

Twenty minutes later I pried myself off the floor long enough to take a shower and eat breakfast. Though aching from hunger, my will to eat was completely gone. I couldn't force the food down and had to spit it onto the plate. My body and my brain were being taken hostage by something utterly indescribable.

Walking the pace of a sickly snail, I made my way to the subway so I could get to my restaurant job. A five-minute walk became fifteen and I finally made it onto the train as it was about to leave. Extreme nausea set in as the train moved through its next few stops.

Approaching the 72nd Street station, I couldn't hold my composure another minute, so I pushed my way off the train and onto the crowded platform to vomit into a trash can. Wiping my mouth and the tears from my eyes, I called my boss to tell him that I was too sick to come into work.

As I arrived back at my apartment, all I wanted to do was sleep but my mind wouldn't allow it. My thoughts were consumed with Lara, my father, and all things I lacked in my life. A sharp pain pulsated through my body. Inside my brain, the words "death" and "suicide" were flashing in large letters on an electrified neon marquee sign advertising a coming attraction.

I fell back to the hardwood floor in my bedroom, curled up in a fetal position. I stayed there and sobbed for hours—more than I ever had for a broken bone or a dead father.

CRISIS ON THE FOURTH FLOOR

Somehow, I survived for three weeks in this perfectly imperfect storm of despondency, the inability to eat more than one meal a day or sleep more than three hours a night. A terrible pain continued to course through my body and a knot was growing inside me, born of malnutrition and anxiety. I was able to pull off working a few days each week, but not without questions of why I looked so ill—questions I wouldn't and couldn't dignify with a response.

In late January I had four scheduled days off in a row from work and nothing to do but stay inside my apartment.

The first three days were a blur. I stopped showering and didn't even leave my bedroom. On the fourth day I decided it was time to make it to the bathroom and clean the stink off my body that now smelled like a cross between a sweaty foot and rancid taco meat.

For the first time in four days I looked at myself in the bathroom mirror. My eyes were bloodshot and my skin lily white save for a few blotches of pink and yellow that gave a more complete color palette. My stomach was sore from hunger as well as the ever-expanding knot growing within its core. Compassion for the man in the mirror quickly soured to displeasure and disgust. I didn't know this pathetic piece of a man anymore and I couldn't stand the pain any longer.

(—*It's okay, homie. You don't have to feel like this anymore.—*)

(—*Si, papa. Estas completo. You're finished.—*)

(—*And it came to pass that none had wept when thou hadst died. Go.—*)

I found myself backing away from the mirror and moved my body back through the doorway and over to my bedroom window.

In front of my fourth floor window was a radiator too hot to touch from the steady flow of heat emanating from its center. My bare feet found a pair of slippers lying alongside my bed and I carefully stepped onto the radiator. The bottom opening of the window was protected by rusty bars fastened to the window's frame but the top was free. I pulled it down till both top and bottom portions of the window were aligned and the hole on top was large enough for me to pass through.

I pushed my head through the opening and looked out at the building across the street. It was singed from a fire that nearly destroyed its top three floors a few months prior and whose smell of ashes made its way to my nostrils whenever the window was open and the wind was blowing in just the right direction.

With my large head still protruding through the opening, I gaped at the sidewalk lined with cars and heaps of trash spilling into the street four stories below. My hands were now sweating profusely and my mind swirling with logic mixed with the devilish little voices.

(—I can't go headfirst. It'll ruin my face.—)

(—*An open casket funeral is the least of your concerns, homie.*—)

(—No. I'm going out backwards. I'm doing this the right way.—)

I turned my body around and lifted myself to where I was sitting on the window's opening. However, the logistics of maneuvering my head and hips out the window at the same time proved to be an impossible feat so I gave up. I turned around and started to go out the front by pushing my head and chest out the window.

My arms shook like weeping willow trees in the middle of a violent tornado. The wind was whipping around something fierce. Tears dribbled every which way across my face, wetting the hair on my temples. With my left hand I supported the weight of my body and with the right, I slapped myself repeatedly. My temples were now completely soaked. With the right hand back in place, I hoisted my torso halfway through the window. But before I could pass all the way through, a strange and unfamiliar voice spoke to me. It was powerful yet tender and barely audible.

(—Josh... Josh... Joshua.—)

(—What? What!?—)

(—*This isn't the way. This isn't your time.*—)

(—What am I supposed to do? I'm hurting. I can't do this anymore.—)

(—*You don't have to. Go back inside. Go back inside and ask for help.*—)

(—From who? Who's going to help me?—)

(—*Go back inside and ask for help.*—)

A Seat on the Fence between Life and Death

I held myself suspended for a few more moments, my body halfway out the bedroom window. I then climbed back through and sat beside the radiator.

To whom could I turn to ask for help? I hadn't asked for anything from anyone in a very long time, maybe decades. It was a matter of pride. I had paid my own way for everything since I was fifteen years old. But if I didn't ask for help here, my pride was going to get me killed.

And, so I spoke aloud, "What am I doing? How am I going to ask for—I don't know. God. God? We haven't talked in awhile. I'm not even sure what to say. I need help. I need help. I can't stop thinking about this girl and my dad and my life and... dying. I don't know what to do. I don't know where to go... I'm just so messed up, goddamn it. I'm sorry I didn't mean to... it's not you, it's me. It's just... I don't know how to ask for help. I don't ask for anything, ever. But... but my dad never asked. And my granddad never asked. So, I have to ask. Help me find somebody or something. Inspiration. I don't know. Just... I can't keep going on like this. Please help me... help me connect to positive people, positive thoughts, positive experiences. Help me connect to positive people, positive thoughts, positive experiences. Positive people, positive thoughts, positive experiences. Positive people, positive thoughts, positive experiences. Positive people, positive thoughts, positive experiences."

An hour of that audible repetition put the voices in my head on mute, clarity that gave way for some serious debate about who or where I could turn to for help.

"I don't have too many friends and God knows if they could handle the weight of this. I can't call Lara. She'll get mad at me. I can't... wait, wait... I know who to call. It's a stretch but she—no, I *can't*. But she knew what he was going through at the end. I'll do it. I'll call her. We'll just have to see what happens."

So, I called my mother. The person who gave birth to me, raised me, and then completely betrayed me. But none of that mattered anymore. She knew my father and she knew me all too well. Maybe there was something she could do or say that would make it all better, like when I was a little boy. I just wanted my mommy.

THE DEATH OF A PRIDEFUL MAN

The phone must have rung fifteen times before her coworker picked up and told me she was out of the office. She asked if I wanted to leave a message.

"Yes, it's her son and I'm thinking about killing myself. Would you please make sure she gets that?" There was no way I was leaving that message.

"No, I'll call back later."

Desperate and determined to talk to someone, I called my mother's cell phone.

Ring.

(—*Papi, you get back up on that radiator.*—)

Ring.

(—I don't know if I can do that.—)

Ring.

(—*It isn't a request, homeboy. That radiator.*—)

Ring.
(—Is way too hot. And I can't go out like that.—)

Ring.

(—*Trust and obey.*—)
Ring.

(—Shut the fuck up!—)

Ring.

"Hi, Josh. This is a nice surprise. How are you?" my mother asked.

"Um hi... not so good," I said in a hushed staccato voice.

"What's going on Josh?"

"I don't know how to tell you this... but I just need to talk to you. I need you to listen and please... I don't even know if I want any advice but I'm in a bad place right now. All I can do is think of Lara and... all day and all night. I can't eat and I can't sleep. I'm obsessing over this girl. I messed things up with her and I messed up my life and I have nothing and nowhere to go and I think I might feel like Dad did. He couldn't stop thinking about you..."

"Are you thinking of... are you thinking of suicide?" she asked. Her voice trembled in fear that her eldest boy was, in fact, very much her dead husband's son—a boy who might end his life before he could produce another heir to enter into this wretched cycle of death.

I grew silent, not ready to admit the truth, fearful of whatever would come next if I did. But the mystery of the unknown wasn't nearly as bad as the pain, sadness, and guilt that was wreaking havoc on my brain and the rest of my body.

"Yes. Yes I am. I think I might do what... Dad did. I don't want to but all I ever do is lay on my floor and cry *all* the time. I need help. I don't know what to do but I need you to say something."

And she paused ever so briefly. I could hear her stifle tears.

"Joshua, I love you very much. You know your life is important to me. I know we don't hold the same beliefs... but maybe this is God telling you that you need to come back to Him, to come back to church—"

"Mom, this ISN'T the time for that. I don't need to hear that right now. I just need some practical advice. I need to know that I can call you and you won't lecture me, or else I'll hang up."

"No, you're right, Josh. You can call me anytime and I will listen," she said with a trace of panic in her voice. "How serious are these thoughts you've been having?"

"I don't know. I almost... I don't really want to die, but I don't know what else to do."

"Do you... have pills in your apartment or anything else you can hurt yourself with?"

"No, no, of course not." I hadn't even thought about that. All I had was a radiator and slippers.

"Listen, maybe you should talk to a professional. Maybe a psychologist or something like that."

Hearing her suggest a psychologist surprised me. Most church folk I knew would tell me to go to the pastor and pray about it with him. Bring your cares to *Jeeee*-sus.

"You're probably right. I've been meaning to look into talking to someone."

"I know you're thinking about, you know... but... is there any reason or reasons you might want to live?"

"I think so. I'm pretty sure now that you mention it."

"That's good Josh. Do you want to talk about them with me?"

"I think... I want to keep that private for a little while. I'd be too embarrassed..." I said, trailing off into pensive deliberation as to whether my potential reasons for living were even worth the trouble.

"Do you think after we get off the phone you could sit down and write out what those reasons might be?"

"Yes. Yes, I can do that," I said. We were having a real conversation and she actually cared about me. The icicles that had formed over her place in my heart were thawing.

"That's very good. I'm very proud of you."

"Thank you and, um, on the God stuff... I did say a prayer recently. I felt pretty good about it."

"That sounds good. It certainly couldn't hurt."

"Thank you. And thanks for listening."

"Anytime, Josh. You know that you can call me anytime, day or night."

"Yeah, thanks. Listen I'm gonna come down and see you and everyone this weekend. Okay? But I should let you go..."

"Okay. I love you Josh."

"I... love you too."

While sitting at my desk, I wrote out my reasons for wanting to live on a blank piece of white printer paper.

1) I'll feel so guilty. If I kill myself, Erica and Jacob will probably be

very upset. I can't let them lose their father and their brother... not like this.

2) There could be other adventures, many of them which I'll never experience... Macchu Picchu. Hawaii. Antarctica. Outer space.

3) A family of my own. A soul mate... a happily ever after, a fairytale ending...

After reading and re-reading what I wrote, I folded the paper eight times till it fit into my wallet—a place where I could quickly find those reminders whenever my thoughts directed me to self-implode.

Finishing up at my desk, I staggered over to my bed to lie down, exhausted from all of the emotional and physical activity of the day. I had a lot to process: my three reasons to live, seeking professional help, and getting better. I wasn't going to die that day, not by my own hands. How I would live— that was another story.

JOSH RIVEDAL

THIRTY-SIX

LIVING OFF THE LAND

The morning after my near suicide attempt, I woke with the sun shining directly onto my face with a cold breeze circulating through the room. I had forgotten to close the window and pull the shade down before I went to sleep. That simultaneous feeling, the severe contrast between cold and hot on my face was a harsh reminder of yesterday's cerebral battle between life and death.

At once, I jumped out of bed and pushed up on the window to close it, as if I was racing to shut out the memories with it, the pain and truth of the prior day and the possibility of a relapse. It wouldn't be that easy. I keeled over and cried while clenching my torso, touching the mango-sized knot that had swelled inside my stomach from weeks of barely eating.

"God, please help me think positive thoughts! Help me connect to positive people! And help me connect to positive experiences!" I prayed in a voice most raucous, covering my mouth with a large pillow to prevent my roommates from hearing my cries. I repeated that prayer out loud for nearly a half hour till my head was clear enough to start my day. I needed a shower. I smelled like bag of rotten turkey giblets from not having cleaned myself in four days.

Following my shower, I went straight for the wallet sitting on my desk and from it I removed the white piece of paper I had scribbled on the night before. I carefully unfolded it eight times and read to myself repeatedly the three reasons why I wanted to live. It wasn't helping and so, once again, I began to repeat my new mantra:

"God, please help me think positive thoughts."

(—*These aren't going to do you any good, homie...*—)

"Help me connect to positive people."

(—*Papi, eschucha, no one cares if you live or die...*—)

"And help me have positive experiences."

This was truly survival mode. All other activities—playwriting, acting, waiting tables—were all put on hold until I could figure out how to stay alive without cycling through obsessive thoughts about my death. Eating, sleeping, and working were all foreign concepts that I had to relearn. Continuous cycles of repeating my mantra and reading my one-sheet of reasons to live helped me make it through those first few days.

BY ANY MEANS NECESSARY

It had been about a week since my decision to stay alive when I found the strength and focus to begin researching what was causing me to become a mental and physical invalid. There had to be an explanation, or some kind of public record of other people living (or dying) through the same painful sensations I was feeling throughout my brain and body. I wanted to call it "depression" but was it something more?

I flipped open my laptop and Googled "depression." There were over two hundred million search results. "Major Depression" was one of the first links to appear.

Click.

"DEPRESSION MAY BE DESCRIBED AS FEELING
SAD, BLUE, UNHAPPY, MISERABLE, OR DOWN IN
THE DUMPS. MOST OF US FEEL THIS WAY AT ONE
TIME OR ANOTHER FOR SHORT PERIODS."

(—Most of us? This is the first time I'm hearing
about it.—)

"TRUE CLINICAL DEPRESSION IS A MOOD DISOR-
DER IN WHICH FEELINGS OF SADNESS, LOSS, AN-
GER, OR FRUSTRATION INTERFERE WITH
EVERYDAY LIFE FOR WEEKS OR LONGER."

(—So I might have "clinical" depression? Dude,
that sounds bad.—)

"...THE EXACT CAUSE OF DEPRESSION IS NOT
KNOWN. MANY RESEARCHERS BELIEVE IT IS
CAUSED BY CHEMICAL CHANGES IN THE BRAIN.
THIS MAY BE DUE TO A PROBLEM WITH YOUR
GENES—"

(—Thanks, Dad. You are truly the gift that keeps
on giving.—)

"—OR TRIGGERED BY CERTAIN STRESSFUL
EVENTS... MORE LIKELY, IT'S A COMBINATION OF
BOTH... BREAKING UP WITH A BOYFRIEND OR
GIRLFRIEND... DEATH OR ILLNESS OF SOMEONE
CLOSE TO YOU..."

(—Yeah, how about all of that stuff at once?—)

"SYMPTOMS OF DEPRESSION CAN INCLUDE: BE-
COMING WITHDRAWN OR ISOLATED, DRAMATIC
CHANGE IN APPETITE, FEELINGS OF SELF-HATE—"

(—Are they reading my mind?—)

"—LOSS OF INTEREST OR PLEASURE IN ACTIVI-
TIES THAT WERE ONCE ENJOYED,—"

(—Like leaving the apartment, booze, sex, and
show business?—)

"...AND THOUGHTS OF SUICIDE."

Fantastic. Self-diagnosis complete. At least I
wasn't crazy. They never even mentioned that
word. I was dealing with some sort of depression.
Now I had to find a way to get rid of it. Advice
from several other official-looking websites men-

tioned that one could prevent depression by staying away from drugs and alcohol, by getting exercise, and by talking about their feelings with someone they trust. Whatever it took. Hell, if they said that watching a twenty-four-hour marathon of *Barney & Friends* while tripping on acid prevented depression, I would have done it.

So, I pulled out my ten-pound barbells from underneath my desk and wiped away the dust caked on them from months of inactivity. I threw out all of my beer and flushed all of my marijuana down the toilet. Then, I made a list of all my trusted family members and old friends whom I could force myself to reconnect with and talk to if I found myself in need of help.

That night and for the first time in weeks, I fell into a deep sleep. I even got a visit from someone whose face I had grown accustomed to but whom I hadn't seen in a few weeks.

THIRTY-SEVEN

···

I WISH I KNEW HOW TO QUIT YOU

It was night. I would have been surrounded by nothing but pitch-black if not for the incandescence of a full moon. The rainforest was still intact but it was now winter and pure white snow coated the entire ground. All the trees had icicles hanging from them instead of leaves, save for a few evergreens clumped together off in the distance.

I was certainly dressed for the occasion with a snowsuit, boots, mittens, and a thick skullcap that covered my ears. A ball of light began to emanate from the singular patch of evergreen trees. I sprinted toward it at full speed to see what was illuminating the forest in such an artificial way.

The closer I got to the only patch of green in the forest, the more the ball of light dimmed.

When I got to its source, I found Ghost Dad, in one of the trees (a Douglas fir I presumed) sitting on a flimsy low-lying branch.

"Where have you been!?" I asked. I was outraged.

"You need to keep going—"

"You abandoned me—*again!*" I yelled.

"I've been with you the whole time." His voice didn't raise in the slightest.

"I'm quitting. I'm not going to tell your story," I said without any remorse.

"You can't."

"I don't care what's in it for me anymore," I bellowed, while frozen tears crystalized in streams down my cheeks.

"That is perfect." He spoke calmly and with a slight smile.

"I don't understand."

"Goodbye."

And with that the ball of light reappeared and expanded to the size of a New York City skyscraper until it imploded. After my dead father disappeared, so did the rainforest and in its place were green digital numbers in a grey plastic box that read 9:00.

THIRTY-EIGHT

·······································

TAMING THE BEAST WITHIN

M y morning began with a shower, a reading of the tattered paper with the three reasons for living, and the recitation of more mantras to drown out the demons who persisted in testing my limits each and every minute of every single day.

"Help me think positive thoughts."

(—*You're gonna snap at some point, dawg. When you do, we'll be here.*—)

"Help me connect to positive people."

(—*I am familiar in all your ways. You are unloved.*—)

"And help me have positive experiences."

(—*In your dreams, pendejo. Matarse. Die.*—)

I needed to know how common it was for people to go through clinical depression because I was feeling like a bit of a social outcast. No one I ever knew talked about feeling like this. I had heard people say they were "depressed" when the Cleveland Browns fielded another losing team or when *The Fresh Prince of Bel-Air* went off the air, but they weren't lining up to jump out of their bedroom windows either. I wanted—no needed—some reassurance that I wasn't a complete freak, and so I found myself researching depression and suicide once again.

Within a few days I read hundreds of stories about people dealing with depression. Many of them had experienced similar feelings as I did, and suffering from the same lack of desire to engage in activities we once enjoyed. The first "normal" thing I started to miss and wanted back was writing. I hadn't written a word since November, more than three months, and putting my thoughts to paper felt like a good way to alleviate my mental and physical pain. I decided to pen something like a diary or blog, addressed to an audience of no one.

A Daily Survival Guide

Dear Friends,

My name is Josh, and I may have been battling some kind of depression for most of my life, but recently it got to be unbearable. I am writing because I want to find a way to help life get better, and I want to help other people at the same time by talking about my experiences. Maybe it will help. Somehow life has to get better and I aim to figure out how with your help.

A little about me. I'm in my late twenties. I have had some major suicidal thoughts at times throughout this period. Thank God that I haven't had the "cojones" to go through with it.

I lost my father and grandfather to suicide. Maybe it's taboo to talk about it, but if you have a history of mental illness in your family, tell your kids so they can get the help they need. I keep reading that 1 in 10 Americans are living with depression or 1 in 5 or 1 in 2, depending on the source.

Any of those figures represent a lot of people who are sad. Can we as a species come together somehow and figure out how to make things better for each other and ourselves? I don't know but I'm going to try and it starts with this blog.

Love,
Josh

"The miracle is not to fly in the air, or to walk

on the water, but to walk on the earth."
-Chinese Proverb

My take on this: It's a pretty big miracle that
we're alive today. We were born and our parents chose life for us. It's a miracle that our
lungs expand and fill with air and that our legs
move and we can walk around. I'm going to try
to carry that simple idea around with me for
the day.

* * *

Strangling the Life Out of My Depression was the name
of my new survival guide. Writing was part of a
new daily regimen, diverting my attention away
from feelings of self-hate and despair and toward
new, positive ideas. The alcohol and pot were easy
habits to quit. I had gotten rid of them before and
they weren't the kind of friends I needed at a time
like this. Never much of a gym guy, a few repeti-
tions with my ten-pound barbells, a set of fifty
pushups, and walks down Riverside Drive sufficed
as my workout regime. I started visiting old
friends—my hippie friend David, my former
roommate Steve, and Namakula, the webisode director. Most of my trips were to New Jersey to
hang with my buddy Zach who I met on the
freshman high school football team.

As fourteen-year-old boys, we bonded over our mutual athletic suckiness, our existential conversations about whether Diet Dr. Pepper really does taste like regular Dr. Pepper, and our ability to overcome our differences—his staunch atheism and my hardcore African Voodooism (or rather dogmatic Christianity). In the years post high school we stayed in touch sporadically yet still maintained a friendship. In the weeks after my near suicide attempt, he became my unofficial *consigliere*, with words of wisdom like, "Don't beat yourself up, Josh"; "Focus on the good stuff, Josh"; and "You might want to slap a little deodorant on, Josh."

As I was coming out of my funk (see: dejected, non-George Clinton type), I needed my tattered printer paper less and less. The combination of friends, praying, and exercise had suppressed my thoughts of dying. The fickle and sometimes deleterious voices in my head were gradually mellowing out. The knot in my stomach was a mere lump of coal in my stomach. Eating wasn't as much of a chore and my usual voracious appetite for fast food and anything that included bacon was starting to return. Ghost Dad hadn't appeared since I had happened upon him sitting in the Douglas fir tree.

A Rich Man Is a Family Man

Dear Friends,

Today I'd like to focus on how I am feeling a little better. I'm not all the way there yet but hopefully this is the start of a prolonged period of non-depression. I visited my mom and brother last night and stayed over into the morning. It was nice to go there and talk with them and have their support. For the first time in years I am finding a connection with them.

I guess I'm mentioning all this because I'm seeing a correlation between finding people who are supportive of you and how you feel about yourself (your mental health) in the day to day. As I'm going through the worst period of my life, I am going to try to keep connecting with the positive people and get rid of the negative people who have the potential to bring me down or keep me in my state of depression.

Love,
Josh

"I don't care how poor a man is; if he has family, he's rich."
-Dan Wilcox and Thad Mumford, "Identity Crisis," episode of M*A*S*H

My take on this: It may seem silly to include a quote from an episode of MASH (Dan Wilcox and Thad Mumford were the executive story editors on the show) but as I was looking for a quote to include today, this one stuck with me more than any other. Family doesn't have to be a blood relative. It can be your college roommate, people from church, your support group or any other place where you feel a positive reciprocal connection to someone. By having these people in our lives we are truly rich. And if you don't have anyone or haven't connected with your family or friends or anyone in a while, maybe try to reach out and connect or reconnect. It is my feeling that these are the people who will help us in our day-to-day fight with depression.

* * *

Little by little I found the strength to search for a new career to pursue, something that would make me happy; something to replace acting and show business. The only requirements I had for my new and undetermined line of work were: that it had nothing to do with fame, had to include writing, and had to help other people. Too many years were wasted worrying whether or not I was going to get some dinner theatre job in Wisconsin, or hoping to win a role as the next rookie detective paired with Jerry Orbach on Law & Order.

DETECTIVE RIVEDAL REPORTING FOR DUTY

INT. LT. VAN BUREN'S OFFICE - DAY

Detective Briscoe, still in his trench coat with a coffee in hand, stands with his mouth agape alongside two dumbstruck police officers in their uniform blues.

A camera pans briefly to what they're staring at — the face of a dead Detective Ed Green hanging from a noose.

> BRISCOE
> Somebody cut him down, will ya? He shouldn't be left here like this.

> COP # 1
> Why would he do it, Lenny?

> BRISCOE
> What if *he* didn't do it?

> COP # 2
> You saying you think this is a homicide?

> BRISCOE
> What else could it be? His little girl was born yesterday… he was the happiest I'd ever seen him.

Just then, a baby-faced cop in an oversized trench coat rushes in. He is quite disheveled, out of breath, and is wearing fresh coffee stains down the front of his shirt, tie, and trench coat.

                    RIVEDAL
Hey everyone, sorry I'm late. Detective
Josh Rivedal reporting for my first day.
I'm here from Boise. What did I miss?

                    BRISCOE
Lenny Briscoe. What did you miss? Are
you blind from gorging your face on all
those Idaho potatoes? My partner… Ed,
he's dead.

                    RIVEDAL
I'm so sorry. Is it… self-inflicted?

                    BRISCOE
We think it's a homicide.

                    RIVEDAL
Any leads?

                    BRISCOE
No, genius, your guess is as good as
mine.

Suddenly, Rivedal sees an envelope peering out from underneath Lt. Van Buren's
desk. A camera zooms in for a close up
on the envelope as Rivedal reaches down
to pick it up.

                    RIVEDAL
(Reads) From Ed to Lenny. (To Briscoe)
Hey Lenny, here's something you might
want to check out. It might give us a
clue as to why Ed is… hanging around…

Dissolve to black. The sound of the Law
& Order "Clang-Clang" is heard. The
opening credits play.

REWRITING THE INTERNAL SCRIPT

How did people ever change careers prior to the advent of the World Wide Web? If I had my suicidal pseudo-nervous breakdown in that dark Mesozoic period pre-1989, I would be doomed to flipping burgers between extra work on internet soap operas for the rest of my meager existence.

Millions of people's brains and bodies were being ravaged by depression and no one was talking about it. Could talking, could my introspective little diary be the thing to fill the void and help other people suffering from depression and other mental illnesses? People like me, needed to know that they were not alone. If no one else wanted to do it, then I would be the William Wallace of depressed people everywhere. "You may be able to take our appetite and our ability to sleep through the night... but you'll never take OUR FREE WILL!! Through the collection of a community we could be *Winning the War on Depression,* which became the new title of my diary.

After completing my psychotic, Scottish, Mel Gibson rant, I turned my focus to what I really wanted most out of life: to feel some sort of happiness, the kind that seemed to elude me, my entire life.

The current state of my happiness, had to be exclusively tied into moving further away from depression. Hours turned into days spent rummaging through Google searches on "how to be happy." Websites, blogs, and chat rooms were filled with rhetoric like: happiness wasn't some sort of an endpoint but the journey in getting there, and happiness wasn't some fast acting magic pill, it was a lifestyle that needed constant maintenance.

A few of the blogs I had started reading, discussed something called "Practicing Gratitude"—an intriguing but far-fetched liberal concept with which I was unfamiliar. Practicing gratitude was simply the idea that to cultivate true happiness, one needed to consistently, and with some effort, count their blessings, employing a glass-half-full mindset every single day. By making it a priority to focus on even the smallest benefits in your life, it was supposed to take away the urge to pay constant attention to your burdens. This wouldn't be the easiest ideal to put into practice when I had been letting little monsters of self-sabotage run wild and free in my brain for most of my life. But the people writing about it seemed legitimately content with their lives, and explained it without any of the dogmatism I'd seen throughout my childhood, I decided to add it to my daily rituals and prayers.

"Thanks for my bed, my family, my friends, that I'm alive, that I'm able to write, that I have Netflix, that I'm less depressed, for the sweet voices of John Legend and Adele, and thank you for the sunshine." Humming the *Golden Girls* theme song while I said my prayers made the activity a self-entertaining event.

The Whispered Words of Wisdom

Dear Friends,

I've been thinking about the power of music and how it can heal. I've been on a Beatles kick recently after watching a YouTube clip of Paul McCartney receiving a Kennedy Center Honor. And I keep listening to the classic, "Let it Be," over and over. Hitting the lowest of lows during my battle with depression, when I put that song on it comforted me in a way that I'd never experienced before. The lyrics speak to me in a deep way.

As I'm going through a difficult time in my life and going through change, I am seeing that I need to "let things be." I need to be gentle and not fight and just go with the flow. Ride the wave so to speak. Things will work out if I stop and look around and let them be.

There's also this 'Mother Mary,' giving advice in one's hour of darkness, the idea of which is quite soothing. When I was in need, my 'Mother Mary' was my own mother, God, and some of my good friends. I'm very lucky to have those people in my life and if you take the time to look around, you'll find the 'Mother Mary' in your life too.

* * *

Classes at Baruch College soon reconvened. I signed up for only two: Great Works of Literature and Calculus I in order to challenge and develop the left and right sides of my brain equally. The routine of academia was a welcome change of pace that kept my thoughts occupied, but not completely distracted or free from momentary lapses of despair and self-doubt.

I hadn't seen Ghost Dad in my dreams in awhile but it was only a matter of time before he appeared again, especially since I had retired from show business effectively putting our *Gospel* away for good. For once, I missed his familiar presence.

One Sunday in early February, I was on my lunch break sitting in a hallway in the basement of my restaurant job. I was positioned in between the employee coat check station and one of the exit doors that led to the trash depot.

Leaning back in a green leather bound chair with only three working legs, I started retracing each twist and turn my life had taken in the past two years. And then I started to consider what I was going to do with the rest of my life. I wanted— no needed—to help people in some way. At the same time, it occurred to me that I was beginning to long for a piece of my life that had meant so much to me for a very long time—a piece I was currently avoiding—show business. How strange. I had completely disavowed that as part of a self-absorbed former life.

I was happy to call myself a former actor. Early morning auditions, rejection, and abject poverty were awful ways to eke out an existence. However, there were those times, few and far between, when the stars aligned and I would get hired in a good role and get to work on great material. Performing on a giant stage, playing make believe for eight shows a week in front of hundreds of people was an otherworldly phenomenon of pure magic. But those were thoughts I had to put away in the damp, dark cellar of my mind. They were a thing of the past. It was a shame I couldn't do creative work like that while helping people at the same time. But these thoughts were put on hold as I felt myself drifting off into sleep.

THIRTY-NINE

A SHARP PAIN

This time I was sitting in the Douglas Fir. Across from me in another tree branch was none other than my Patriarchal Sandman.

"You're looking much better," he stated.

"Thank you, I'm trying..."

"You are not trying hard enough," he said, his voice becoming hostile.

"But I need to take care of myself..."

"It's all right under your nose."

"Can't you just tell me what I need to know? Please." I begged.

"It won't be the same. It's time to go."

We parted ways. He disappeared, and I woke with a sharp pain at the front of my forehead. A second chair leg had given way, causing my body to propel forward head first into the white painted stone wall in front of me.

FORTY

....

A SMACK-ON-THE-NOGGIN EPIPHANY

Maybe it was the dream or maybe it was the smack on my noggin, but it finally came to me—it was all in front of me. I was going to combine show business, my desire to help people, and my dead father's edict to tell his story—a new triumvirate with whom I could have a much healthier relationship.

The Gospel According to Josh included several scenes about my father's suicide at the end of the show. I could use my own experience to give away life-saving information about suicide and prevention that my grandfather and father never had. Truly a 21st century William Wallace fighting alongside those souls fed up paying homage to two feudal lords, enchainers known as Silence and Depression.

In that basement hallway, smarting from a smack on the skull, I ended my brief retirement from show business. My brief hiatus didn't provide me with nearly enough time to try and fail at any other careers like semi-professional baseball like my childhood idol, Michael Jordan (Go Birmingham Barons!). *The Gospel According to Josh* combined with suicide education and awareness would be my welcome back tour. The only thing left to do was find a new work jersey displaying the number "45" to wear for the next few weeks.

Time to put my eureka moment into action and see if it could actually work outside of the confines of my bruised cranium and in the real world. I didn't just *want* to do a one-man show combined with suicide prevention. I needed to do it for my own sanity. I needed to be responsible for people other than myself. I needed it to help me stay alive.

....

FORTY-ONE

THE NEW NORMAL

Having some kind of potential life-changing epiphany did not mean I was out of the woods with my recovery.

Psalm 23

Dear Friends,

Today as I was sitting on the subway on my way to work I was thinking about my depression and how dark things had gotten for a while. I was feeling pretty anxious, like I could easily slip down that black hole again. But out of nowhere, some familiar words from my childhood popped into my head: "Yea, though I walk through the valley of the shadow of death, I will fear no evil: for thou art with me; thy rod and thy staff they comfort me." That beautiful poetry eased my fears and gave me real encouragement.

In case you didn't know, it's from Psalm 23 in the Christian Bible. I hadn't picked up a Bible or thought of that verse in years and it came to me at just the right time. I have been walking in the valley of the shadow of death. And I realized that as I was going through losing my father, family turmoil, a lousy break up, and my own struggle with depression, there's been some kind of a higher power looking out for me. And I totally forgot that:

The Lord is my shepherd; I shall not want. 2 He maketh me to lie down in green pastures: he leadeth me beside the still waters. 3 He restoreth my soul: he leadeth me in the paths of righteousness for his name's sake. 4 Yea, though I walk through the valley of the shadow of death, I will fear no evil: for thou art with me; thy rod and thy staff they comfort me. 5 Thou preparest a table before me in the presence of mine enemies: thou anointest my head with oil; my cup runneth over. 6 Surely goodness and mercy shall follow me all the days of my life: and I will dwell in the house of the Lord forever.

THE DATING GAME

While still emerging from my depressive state I was determined to make an effort to jump into the dating field—for love, for a distraction, and to prevent penis-atrophy. Since I had temporarily quit drinking in January, I didn't have the assistance of copious amounts of Heineken to aid my conversations with attractive women. As a result, I reverted back to being god-awful at it. Even the sight of one brought on a horrifying fit of temporary amnesia. Somehow I could never remember my name, my astrological sign, or who was president. And when I was able to open my mouth it was only to insert my own foot.

After a frustrating cycle of failed dating attempts, I did what every socially awkward man in his late-twenties does who desperately misses the sweet touch of a woman—I forked over a hundred bucks and joined a dating website. I knew quite a few people who had found their long-term significant other thanks to the world of online dating. If those ogreish freak-shows could make it work typing on their keyboards while nestled in safely behind their computers (probably in their pajamas and eating a pint of Rocky Road) then so could I. Armed with the unlimited use of a thesaurus and a backspace button, I launched my campaign.

I uploaded one of my acting headshots for a profile picture. Nothing says "confident bad-boy" like having your picture taken wearing a five o'clock shadow in front of a rusty chain link fence. Nothing says "sweetheart" like having the Shakespeare quote, "Love all. Trust a Few. Do Wrong to None," as your profile headline. With the benefit of retrospect, that quote probably made me look like a promiscuous guy with trust issues. It'sJustForTonight.com.

My only criteria for a match was that it be a woman between the ages of twenty-one and thirty with no children. While I was usually a vanilla guy, in the spirit of turning over a new leaf I was willing to try new flavors like mocha, pecan, dark chocolate, and any kind of Asian except that weird girl that lived on the second floor of my apartment building.

Navigating the world of online dating came with a bit of a learning curve. The first judgment of character (and line of defense) was on the quality of a woman's pictures. I figured that any woman with a blurry photo probably looked like the Phantom of the Opera in person. Any woman wearing a baggy t-shirt with her bikinied friends at the beach had to be pregnant. Candids of her and her preschool class were obnoxious and unethical (those children didn't sign waivers to have their likenesses used so their teacher could get laid).

Truly excommunicative offenses included: complaining about her ex-boyfriend(s) and listing *Real Housewives of Omaha* under "Favorite Things."

Everyone was in love with animals, traveling, spending time with family, giving their all to their friends, the belief in modern-day chivalry, and the need for someone to make them laugh. Online dating was even more difficult than the face-to-face kind. Women and a few androgynous men e-winked at me without saying a word (what was I supposed to do with that?). All of the email messages I sent out went unreturned. Internet dating seemed to be all about verbal masturbation and everyone else was getting off except for me.

While I was still navigating the new scenery and set of this new romantic stage, I was excelling at Baruch, still writing daily, and seeing family or friends at least once a week. The only incomplete I had on my to do list was developing a concrete way to act on my smack-on-the-noggin epiphany.

One night in late February, in the middle of getting the first good night's sleep in a long while, I got a visit from someone I hadn't seen for a few weeks.

FORTY-TWO

A GHOST NO MORE

The rainforest was its usual lush, green, and wet self. I stood by my lonesome underneath the same towering Douglas fir as I had before. The sun was shining abnormally bright through the needles of the tree. One particularly vivid and sparkling ray of light, filled with the spectrum of every color in the rainbow, shone through, starting a small brush fire only a yard from where I was standing. It took but a moment for the flames to reach eye level and from them emerged the phantasm of my dead father.

For the first time since our rainforest meetings, Ghost Dad's feet were touching the ground. He plodded toward me with conviction in each step.

"Hello son," said my dead father, wearing a look of relief across his face, something I hadn't seen from this ghost before now.

"Hi," I said.

"I have to leave you now and I can't come back," he confessed, his voice breaking.

"You're leaving again? That's not... " I couldn't finish my sentence. It wasn't fair. I had just gotten used to having him around.

"I am sorry. But you *will* be fine."

"What about your story?" I asked.

"It's bigger than me. You are doing it for them and for you."

"But I'm... I'm going to..." My throat closed up while my tear ducts opened.

"I love you Joshua," he said, pulling me in for an embrace and the proper goodbye we never shared while he was still alive. His grip was so strong that his fingers dug into my rib cage and into the back of my neck. Our cheeks touched and a salty stream of liquid flowed and fused together from each of our eyes.

I held on tight with my eyes closed until I could no longer feel the pain of his fingers pressing into my flesh or his tears running down my face.

FORTY-THREE

WEATHERING THE HIGH SEAS

He was gone and he was never coming back. "God, I'm nervous about all of this... this one-man show stuff. I don't know if I can do it all alone. Please help me."

Whatever my future held, as scary and uncertain as it was, it would never look like the state of my former existence. I couldn't let it. Friends, prayer, and writing all served as integral components of a life raft that took me away from the cold, familiar shores of selfishness, self-loathing and insecurity, and toward a tropical island named Recovery.

As the days turned into weeks, the old shoreline grew ever smaller, and soon enough I found myself in the middle of a cold and violent ocean armed only with my wits and my faith that things could only get better. There was no turning back now. As more time passed my arms grew stronger from persistent rowing. The synapses in my mind fired faster, and my thoughts became sharper without the suffocating and self-medicating agents of Booze, Pot, and Self-Pity that I had been formerly accustomed to.

Thankfully, I wasn't made to take this seafaring journey alone. As I slowly opened up to friends, family, and classmates about my struggle with depression, other brave souls appeared rowing beside me in search of their own new tropical island—some I had known for many years and called friends, and others who became new and invaluable allies. And yes, there were still times when wind and incessant rains threatened to capsize my boat. Praying out loud to the God of the Tempest seemed to help calm the storms. "God thank you for everything that's happened to me—my mom, my dad, my own struggles. Thank you for the wind and the rain. Thank you for my strengths. Thank you for my weaknesses. Help me help others to never have to go through what Dad went through—what I went through. Just please help. Peace."

I soon found that my new journey's endpoint was not simply some shoreline named Recovery.

My journey *was* the recovery. And while there were still so many more storms to weather before finding land, I would never again nourish the demons in my brain with the fodder of negativity or let the will and whims of others direct the course of my ship. This insight made the grueling conditions I endured at sea one of the most productive times of my life. It helped me find my way to aid and support some of the tired, poor, and huddled masses yearning to breathe free from monsters named Depression and Suicide.

··

FORTY-FOUR

THE GOSPEL, SUICIDE PREVENTION, AND A NOSE TO THE GRINDSTONE

"Suicide is a huge but largely preventable public health problem, causing almost half of all violent deaths and resulting in almost one million fatalities every year, as well as economic costs in the billions of dollars"

- THE WORLD HEALTH ORGANIZATION

Preventable? NOT inevitable? Reading the word "preventable" instead of "inevitable" was a watershed moment for me. I had suspected that suicide was genetic due to my family history, and though I had gotten help for it this time, I thought it was something I could only postpone. But discovering that word "preventable" was like receiving a presidential pardon after spending the better part of two years on death row.

"Suicide is the third leading cause of death among 15- to- 24-year-olds, accounting for 12% of deaths in this age group."
- THE TREVOR PROJECT

Suicides by children younger than fifteen are on record, however, the 15- to 24-year-old age group was the earliest age range where suicide became a major issue. That clinched it for me. High school and college students would be my target audience with my *Gospel*. If I could share my story with them, they in turn could carry that information with them for the rest of their lives. And they could spread that same good news to younger generations long after I was dead and gone (from old age, thank-you-very-much).

Time to come up with a game plan—Operation Freedom 2.0. Step 1: Research any and all kinds of entertainment-based youth suicide prevention programming for a little "How To" inspiration.

After hours of research, I only found extremely clinical public service announcements and training programs that were about as engaging as watching someone try to scrape calluses off their old, mangy feet. There was virtually no live entertainment-based programming unless it was related to the very in vogue topic of bullying. However, the layout of one program gave me the answer of how to format my own—a forty-minute version of my one-man show, followed by a twenty-five-minute educational session, and ending with a question and answer period between me, a professional psychologist, and the audience.

Step 2: Understanding depression better and developing concrete learning objectives for my educational *Gospel...* to preempt this venture from becoming artistic masturbation and to insure that audience members could truly find the help they needed. Back to research and the Google grindstone.

The Centers for Disease Control posted a very telling statistic that ninety percent of people who die by suicide have a mental illness present at the time of death. Through countless clinical studies, blogs, and medical journals I found that mental illnesses like depression and post-traumatic stress disorder, among others, are actually treatable chemical imbalances in the brain and not weaknesses of character or anyone's fault. But people weren't getting help for their mental illness because there is tremendous societal stigma attached to it. Even I felt like a bit of a douche bag at first for not being able to shake my depression like any "normal" person would with a hangover or common cold.

My educated but unconfirmed guess about my father's plight was that he unknowingly suffered from post-traumatic stress disorder because of his father's suicide and his forty-three years of shame and silence about the matter. Toward the end of his life, prompted by his divorce, he probably also suffered from clinical depression, manifested in his loss of appetite, sleep, and his isolation from the outside world.

There seemed to be several complicated factors at play that prevented him from getting help: a) The previous stigma he felt because of his father's suicide during the 1960s, b) he was a stubborn jackass who liked to do things his own stubborn jackass way, which probably led to c) the difficulty in admitting there was something wrong inside his brain that was causing him to think he needed to kill himself.

His jackassery aside, it became imperative that through my educational program, I had to show that mental illnesses are real illnesses and that they respond to real treatment. If my father had that knowledge, I'm almost certain he would still be alive.

Comfort Does not Equal Success

Dear Friends,

In our daily walk as people we are all faced with opportunities every day—opportunities to grow or regress, to stay or to leave, to shi-ite or get off the pot.

Each opportunity, great or small, requires us to make a decision. Often that decision is gauged on whether or not the outcome will benefit us and how much of a risk is involved. We're naturally attracted to what's more comfortable for us, but is what is most comfortable for us the best thing for us?

Not always.

The achievement of comfort does not equal success. We must always be self-aware and searching for what we want out of our lives and our careers.

Maybe staying in that romantic (or lack thereof) relationship allows you to stay in that apartment, but leaving that person could allow for greater personal growth. The up-front risk is high (homelessness) and nothing is guaranteed but the potential reward is so great you can't and shouldn't pass it up.

I've found when I've jettisoned relationships and jobs that weren't right for me and given up (okay, more like been dragged away from them while kicking and screaming) creature comforts, my long-term needs were met and I was able to achieve what was best for me.

Put simply, I took a risk with my life, and while every day is still a bit of a struggle, I can see it paying off. I'm not sure what the odds are on your risk fail/success rate, but for you, I'm placing my bets on the latter.

* * *

While reflecting on my father's suicide, I wondered if people considering suicide as an option gave any discernible clues to their suicidal thoughts—flashing signs, or even subtle cries for help on the sound frequency of a dog whistle. If there were symptoms, if my family and I knew what to look for, then we could have gotten my father the help he needed. With the click of a few buttons, I located the National Suicide Prevention Lifeline website and an actual list of common signs of those at risk.

1. Talking about wanting to die or to kill oneself.
2. Looking for a way to kill oneself, such as searching online or buying a gun. - **Dad. Me.**
3. Talking about feeling hopeless or having no reason to live.
4. Talking about feeling trapped or in unbearable pain. - **Me.**
5. Talking about being a burden to others.
6. Increasing the use of alcohol or drugs. - **Me.**
7. Acting anxious or agitated; behaving recklessly.
8. Sleeping too little or too much. - **Dad. Me.**
9. Withdrawing or feeling isolated. - **Dad. Me.**
10. Showing rage or talking about seeking revenge. - **Dad**
11. Displaying extreme mood swings.

Through early March and while developing and polishing up my suicide prevention program, I knew it was paramount that I religiously keep up with my mantras, prayers, and practicing gratitude.

The voices in my head, no longer fat from their previous junk food diet of pessimism and fear, were well-toned bastions of optimism. Dinner with friends and family visits kept me regular. And Ghost Dad kept to his word and stopped visiting me altogether.

* * *

Step 3: Find someone to champion my *Gospel* at their high school or college. The most stress-inducing part of this entire process was trying to find and partner with someone—a virtual stranger who thought that theatre combined with suicide prevention was a good idea; someone who would say the magic word "yes" and get the ball rolling at their institution.

I had my doubts. What if the school administrators I reached out to were as scared as I used to be to talk about, shh, the "S" word? What if they didn't care? What if I my smack-on-the-noggin epiphany was nothing more than brash stupidity from a mild concussion? This program was my baby and like any proud parent, I couldn't bear to hear someone tell me that mine was ugly.

For my opening salvo, I sent out an innocuous nine-paragraph, seven-hundred-word email (a clunky, tongue-twisting, short story of sorts) to college psychology professors and high school administrators all across the United States. I sent out about four hundred email messages, and received only three responses—one from a professor at the University of Oregon who thanked me but "couldn't use my services at this time," another who asked me to take him off my email list, and the last one from an administrator in Utah who wrote back that she hoped I "believe in the one, true Gospel." A week's worth of work, roughly forty total hours, and nothing to show for it. My baby was sprouting a unibrow and a snaggle-tooth.

If You're Going Through Hell, Keep Going

Dear Friends,

I've been thinking about a quote I found after struggling a bit in my work this week:

"If you're going through hell, keep going."
-Winston Churchill

In 1940, only a few weeks after Winston Churchill took over as British Prime Minister,

France was defeated by the Nazis leaving Great Britain as the only European superpower to stand and fight against the would-be German occupiers.

In short time, London and parts of southern England were bloodied and beaten to a pulp from the relentless aerial bombings by the Germans.

But Churchill, often considered by historians to be the greatest wartime leader of the twentieth century, would not give up or let his countrymen give into tyranny. His spirit, leadership, and oratory skills helped Britain find their inner strength to band together and find strategic partners who would help them beat the Germans.

On a different scale we all have mini-hells we go through from time to time. It could be as simple (or as complicated) as a relationship in our business or home life, a start-up company beginning to go sour, or a dream not unfolding the way we envisioned. In these moments of hell it's important that we keep going. It's a given that we should look for encouragement from our supporters but we must also ask ourselves important questions—questions that will guide and coach us to victory.

- What's going well? It's important to take stock here. When things aren't going the greatest, it's easy to say that nothing is going right; and it's here that it's easiest to drop what you're doing and give up. Asking this question also allows us to build on the good stuff and make it grow.

- What would I like to see improve? What do I actually want? Do I remember? Or has my goal morphed under the cloudy vision of disappointment? Asking this question gets us back to the basics. Here we can take a fresh look at the gears of the machine that might need a little extra oil.

- Who or what can help me get where I want to go? Pretty self-explanatory. No man is an island and we all need help from someone or something to get where we need to go.

- Who can I help? This is a great way to remind ourselves that this journey isn't all about us. This can be an offering of help beyond the scope of your comfort zone, or it can be a simple wake-up call for you to figure out the value you offer.

- What am I grateful for? Just a good thing to check in with. Even if it's one thing that you're grateful for, it's something that's in your life for a reason and something you've nurtured or attracted to yourself that is a success. Success breeds confidence and confidence is something you need to make it through your mini-hells.

* * *

The following week, I sent out an additional five hundred email messages and this time I didn't receive any responses. Another week wasted. My snaggle-toothed, unibrowed baby was developing a natty red comb-over and a nasty case of stink breath.

"God, I need positive thoughts. I'm slipping here. Am I an idiot for doing this?"

(—*Watch your mouth and just keep plugging away, papi. Sí se puede.*—)

"I need help from someone. A positive person. But what if they don't come?"

(—*Do not be a doubting Thomas. Think of the words of Churchill.*—)

The Gospel According to Josh: A 28-Year Gentile Bar Mitzvah

"We'll try this for one more week and see what happens. Oh, and Amen. Heavenly fist-bump. Thank you."

For my third week of my email bombardment, I cut the length of my letter and sent out another thousand email messages. This time I didn't get any email responses but one phone call while in line at a cafe, waiting for my usual small cup of dark roast coffee, no sugar, no milk.

"Hello, is this Josh?" asked the friendly, native New Yorker sounding voice.

"Uh, yes. This is he."

"My name is David. I'm a psychology professor at Baruch College. I got your message and I like your idea. I think it could be useful for the student body."

"Awesome. Awesome," I answered, pumping my fist in celebration, a cafe performance that alarmed a few patrons and caused me to spill my coffee all over the floor.

"Yes, I guess it is. Can you send me a copy of your play and can we find a time to meet to discuss all of this a little further?"

The following week I met David and his teaching associate Zach in a suite of psychology department offices at Baruch College down on 24th Street and Lexington Avenue in Manhattan. David looked a little young to be a college professor. If I had to guess, he was probably a favorite of the students because of his down-to-earth demeanor and non-traditionally handsome five o'clock shadow—the kind of professor I would aspire to be in another life. Zach was also on the younger side and not a full-professor but looked the part wearing a pair of small-framed glasses and the traditional suit-and-tie ensemble.

David spoke first. "So, Josh, we only have about thirty minutes to speak before we have to get to class. We both enjoyed the script but the real reason for today's meeting is to get to know you a bit better as a person." I think that was code language for, "We want to make sure you're not a flake or a raging sociopath." I proved myself to be neither and secured a second meeting with them.

Smiling Through the Struggle

Dear Friends,

Today was one of the most difficult days I've had in a while. I sat at my desk and looked at all the work I created for myself and felt a deep sense of emptiness. I felt like I'm working my rear end off and I'm not really accomplishing what I want. I'm struggling right now.

Why? I took a somewhat positive meeting a few days back and it sunk in that I've been beating my head against a wall for the past few weeks. I'm fighting and clawing and nothing is sticking.

I almost let myself sink into prolonged melancholy—a place I've visited before—and dwelling there can be a slippery slope for me. So I started self-coaching, as if I were talking to a friend. I encouraged myself and started to write down things that could help me through my current struggle:

1) Find my smile through the struggle: Find things to connect to that are positive—things like good interpersonal relationships, the fact that I have a home, the good qualities about myself, and/or the things with which I am having success.

2) Sit with myself and strategize: See if the path I'm taking is one that I've chosen, one that I've wandered on, or one that I've been pushed on. If I haven't willfully chosen the path I'm on, start looking at steps to put myself on my desired path.

3) See if there's a lesson in the struggle: There's always a positive takeaway from every situation in life. That doesn't diminish the circumstances or the difficulty of what I'm going through; it just means I get to choose how I let the struggle affect me and for how long.

4) Know that this too shall pass: I've struggled before and have gotten through it. How did I manage to fight past the struggle and succeed? I can use what worked before and know that I have the strength and perseverance to get past this obstacle that's causing me to struggle.

Developing tools to overcome adversity is paramount to a successful personal life. You don't have anything if you don't have your (mental) health.

* * *

Exactly one week later, I returned to the suite of offices in the psychology department. David, wearing a fresh batch of his handsome trademark five o'clock shadow, and Zach, wearing an equally fresh made-for-academia suit and tie, started off in unison like a nerdy version of the Doublemint

Twins. "We think it's best—" one chortled while the other one choked. David, who regained his composure first, continued on, "We think it's best if you plan this event for the end of the semester. You can do it through the Baruch College chapter of Psi Chi. It's a psychology club and I'm the advisor." David brought two students on the Psi Chi executive board into his office to meet me and sent us along into the hallway to talk.

The two student executives, a vertically challenged, athletic-looking young man named Gregory, and an attractive bookworm named Ellen, met with me for an hour or so. We made preliminary plans to have my program as an event for the entire student body in a one-hundred-seat lecture hall on the second Tuesday in May.

"I'll work on promoting the event," Ellen promised.

"And I can get the student government involved," Gregory added.

All I had to do to prepare was rehearse the show, create promotional flyers, and find an additional panelist, besides David and Zach, to help with the question and answer portion of the event. Within a month, I enlisted one of the bigwigs at The American Foundation for Suicide Prevention to be a volunteer panelist. My program, my *Gospel*, and my chance to tell the world my father's story, were all back from the dead and on life support. Beep. Beep. Beep.

A Stomach Strong Enough for Discomfort

Dear Friends,

"Do not repeat the tactics that have gained you one victory, but let your methods be regulated by the infinite variety of circumstances."
— Sun Tzu

This week I was thinking a bit about resiliency and change. If you (and me) are looking to do good work within any aspect of your life, it's going to take a stomach strong enough for discomfort and the knowledge that you will be in a constant state of evolution.

The things that were successful for us yesterday won't necessarily work again tomorrow. Our world is always in a state of flux due to the rise and fall of kings, advanced technology, and the natural aging process. We must, at the very least, attempt to keep up and refine ourselves according to our personal values. If we're not evolving and growing, we're sitting still, our collective butt-prints left on the sands of time. The natural progression of self-evolution in an enlightened society seems to go like this:

- Listen and acknowledge what it is that is changing around you.

- Strategize on what adjustment you need to make in response to change. How will you experience growth as a result of the adjustment?

- Develop yourself.

- Launch the new and improved you (or the thing or idea you want to produce to help others) and take risks when sending yourself (or that thing or idea) into the world.

The you that you send out doesn't have to be perfect and there's no guarantee the energy you put out will be perfect BUT if you follow the first three steps, your risk for "failure" will be minimized.

* * *

As the weeks passed, the Baruch Psi Chi student executives kept their word. Ellen got Baruch's school newspaper to run a small ad about *The Gospel According to Josh* near the back page. Gregory talked the Baruch College student body president into sending out a mass email to five thousand students making them aware of the event. I even spent a few hours on the Friday prior to the show plastering every building, hallway, and lobby at the school with my flyers—all of which managed to stay up through the weekend without being torn down or covered up with posters from the Asian Cultural Exchange's upcoming *Dance Dance Revolution* student event.

One Is Enough

It was the day of the show, and ten minutes prior to the event; David, Zach, Gregory and another student made for a four-person audience. Seven minutes till show time and another five people arrived. This was feeling like *deja vu* to my performance at The Media Theatre from November.

(—*Yo, dawg, can we do that Hail Mary thing again?*—)
(—I think you only get one of those if you're not Catholic.—)

With five minutes to go, five of my show business friends showed up making for a healthier fourteen-person audience. With one minute to spare, some snacks were brought in for the attendees, which enticed another twenty-five students to walk through the door. Never underestimate the power of giving something away for free to a broke college student living on student loan money—food, t-shirts, condoms, booze, snap bracelets—it doesn't matter what it is as long as it's free.

Performing a piece of theatre in a lecture hall is a bizarre phenomenon, like going to Sesame Street as a child and seeing Big Bird in the parking lot without his costume head, while holding a lit cigarette in one hand and a liter of Jameson in the other. In a lecture hall, there's no curtain that splits the audience and performer—nothing to separate the real world from the land of heightened make-believe. In a theater, the lights shining are the ones shining on the performer. For the most part, the audience will look like an endless ocean of black with the sounds of an occasional sneeze or errant cell phone ring. An unlit audience is perfect for the performer because he or she can't see who is engaged and who is checking their watch or falling asleep. In a theater, the performer's singular worry is over their performance, not whether Bertha in the front row is going to stop picking her nose.

The overhead lights in this lecture hall, or at least what I was aware of, had only three settings: on, off, and some sort of unhappy medium. I was distracted from the get-go and quite disconcerted to see every face for which I was performing. An extremely attractive girl in the second row was chewing her gum loudly, like a horse on cocaine. Two of my theatre-producer friends sitting in the back seemed like they were enjoying themselves till one of them let out a half muffled yawn that I hoped was from fatigue. A student in the third row, obviously born with some kind of physical and mental disability seemed pleasantly engaged, but consistently clapped at the most inopportune places—like the part where my father once beat me as a child with copper electrical wire, or at the end where I get the news of my father's suicide. But his smile and enthusiasm, genuine or not, did offer me some strength to get through my first collegiate performance.

Following the show, I was told that we didn't have enough time for me to do any kind of speech but there was time for the panelists to answer audience questions. I took my place in front of a lectern and served as moderator of the panel discussion by asking, "What is the difference between clinical depression and having the blues?"

Each panelist interposed with different answers like, "Clinical depression is usually defined as lasting longer than two weeks," and "Clinical depression is a prolonged state of feeling hopelessness and loss of interest in everyday activities."

An older adult audience member's hand darted through the air and without even being acknowledged asked, "If I ask someone if they're thinking of suicide, is it going to make them do it?"

"One hundred percent no," I answered. "When I was going through my difficult time, my mother asked me whether I was thinking of suicide and that didn't make me do anything. In fact it was a gauge or a meter to see how serious I was thinking about it and showed my mother to be a friend."

One petite, mousey young woman mustered everything she had inside her to raise her hand to ask a question. "Knowing what you know about your father and grandfather, can you speak to whether suicide is hereditary or not?" she squeaked.

"You know, and I'm sure our panelists might have something to say about this, but I'm not sure. I've read studies that have argued for and against suicide as being something genetic. But regardless of whether it's hereditary or not, I'm not a slave to my brain or my background. I can fight back," I said, slapping my hand on the lectern, which had turned into a pulpit during this sermonette.

(—*Preach, Brother Josh. Preach!—*)

As I was cleaning up my equipment and bidding my farewells to David, Zach, and a few of my friends, I noticed over my shoulder a young Latino man, who had been very attentive during the show. He was waiting by himself in the front row and motioned to me to speak with him.

"Hey man, how you doing?" I asked while taking a seat next to him.

"I'm good. I liked your presentation," he said with a certain amount of reticence in his voice. Looking into his eyes there was an undercurrent of emotion waiting to be set free.

"Thanks, dude. I saw you out there. Thanks for paying attention," I said with a slight chuckle.

"Definitely. So I wanted to just thank you for doing this."

"No doubt, yo, it was my pleasure. It was fun."

"Yeah, yeah—but, you know I've been like dealing with being depressed, I think like this clinical kind you talked about, for as long as I can remember. I just thought it was normal. But..."

"It's okay, dude. You can say whatever you want to say. It's all good."

"...I want to get help. And I mean, I didn't even know I could. I want to feel better," he said, his eyes welling up with tears. He dabbed at his eyes with his fists before any liquid spilled onto his cheeks.

"Yes, please, man. You can get better. I'm so glad you came today. Do you know where the counseling center is?"

"Yeah, bro. I'm gonna head down there after my next class."

"Cool man. You need someone to go with you? You want me to go?" I asked hoping this kid wouldn't change his mind once we parted ways.

"Nah, I'm alright. I got it."

"Alright, dude, let me know. But thanks for waiting to talk to me. You have a good one and stay alive, brother. Hit me up on Facebook any time if you need anything."

"Okay."

And with that we said goodbye with a half handshake, half hug that guys give to their good guy friends and the occasional stranger.

As he left the room I had to pause and soak in this epic moment. It didn't matter that huge crowds of students weren't banging down the door to get in to see the show; that the lighting in the space was less than ideal; that I was distracted during the show; or that my ego wasn't stroked enough. All of that was insignificant bullshit. This young man was in search of a way to get help, to live, and he found it that day at my show. All of the heart-wrenching, painful ordeals of the past two years with my father, my mother, Lara, and my own bout with depression—it was *all* worth it to help this one young man get help and stay alive. This was the greatest success I had ever had in show business—no, make that the greatest of my life.

FORTY-FIVE

....

AN EPILOGUE PART TWO—A YEAR TO REMEMBER

School was out for the semester and I got "A's" in all my college classes. The knot living in my stomach had vanished completely and life felt more pliant than even before my head-on collision with depression and suicide. The browns, whites, grays, and blacks that had previously colored my world were now intermingled with vibrant blues, greens, yellows, and reds. To put it simply, I looked forward to waking up every morning.

I decided that the duel focus of that summer would be my own mental wellness and friendships, and building the suicide prevention arm of *The Gospel According to Josh*.

I met an enchanting psychologist at Baruch College named Tina. I began to see her as a patient and I joined the ranks of the approximately 25 million Americans who regularly see a psychologist or psychiatrist. It made me feel whole to be able to speak about some of my deepest, darkest secrets to someone who didn't expect anything from me and wasn't passing judgment on me as good or bad. I was simply "Josh" and had the ability to create whatever kind of world I wanted to live in.

OM

A few weeks into my summer break from school, I received a message from a classmate, Stephanie, asking me to join her in attending a Buddhist teaching given by a Tibetan Buddhist by the name of Kravag. Stephanie, an older woman with a chic fashion sense, and platinum blond hair, was someone I bonded with over our mutual love of theatre and private disclosures surrounding various family issues. She remembered I had been reading the Dalai Lama's *The Art of Happiness at Work*, and thought I'd appreciate Kravag's upcoming teaching on self and attachment. I wasn't exactly thrilled about attending services of another branch of organized religion, but the chance to experience a

Buddhist teaching was exotic and my own abridged version of *Eat, Pray, Love.* I agreed to accompany Stephanie to this Buddhist lecture.

I was expecting services to be held at some kind of temple, lavishly ornamented with golden Buddhas and carp ponds. Instead, I arrived at a place whose insides smelled like incense but looked very much like the kind of Protestant church I had known as a child, complete with stiff wooden pews, a pulpit, and a crucifix, sans Jesus, hanging on the wall behind it. I was filled with an uneasy feeling that these Tibetan Buddhists had converted to some mystical form of Christianity and I was secretly being sandbagged into joining them.

Soon after arriving, I found Stephanie in the vestibule, who laughed at my concerns over deceptive evangelical Tibetan monks, and assuaged my fears. "These Buddhists rent the church from a branch of Swedish Protestants who own the space." Tithing and bake sales must not have been paying the bills anymore.

Walking into the auditorium with Stephanie serving as my escort, everyone sitting in the pews made it a point to smile and share awkward, deep eye contact with me until I turned away. It was like they were scanning the depths of my soul through the window of my eyes to determine if I was "one of them." I was back at the church from my childhood but in some kind of parallel universe.

The two of us sat near the front and for a few minutes made small talk with each other in hushed voices until the teacher, Kravag, took his place on stage—the sign that the ceremony was about to begin. I expected to see a frail, ancient Indian man decked in a bright orange robe and dirty sandals, barely able to hold his head up. In his place I was surprised to see a handsome, fit middle-aged Scandinavian man whose close-cropped hair was flecked with salt and pepper. His presence commanded the full attention of the room. Immediately, he instructed his flock, myself, and the other nameless Buddhist neophytes to close their eyes and follow along with him in a chant praising and thanking the almighty Buddha. I found this unexpected pseudo-ecclesiastical ritual quite disenchanting, but I mumbled along in a singsong tone to feign enjoyment to my gracious host seated next to me.

For the next portion of the evening, Kravag, with a soft and sensual adagio voice, directed the crowd of Buddhists to "close your eyes, put your feet flat on the floor, and let the backs of your hands relax on your knees with palms facing up to the ceiling. Breathe from the belly while inhaling and exhaling through the nose and mouth." We were preparing for a meditation—the sort of outlandish thing I had only ever seen on television. Kravag continued on with, "Relax the jaw and breathe evenly."

(—*Yo, that's what she said.*—)

"Sit forward and erect, but not uncomfortably so."

(—Relax, dudes. I'm trying to concentrate.—)

"Rest your spine on the back of the pew, but..."

(—*Su vida, life, it feels calm for the first time in awhile, no?*—)

"... do not focus on any one thought, just on your breath."

(—I don't miss Lara *and* I've got a date with a woman next week.—)

"Stay with it. Notice how it feels..."

(—*Your joy is your strength. Rejoice!*—)

"... if you start to think about people or things, or stresses of the day, acknowledge that and bring it back to your breath. Let everything else float away."

(—Okay, guys, time to go away. I'll talk to you later.—)

As Kravag continued to guide the congregation through the meditation, my mind and body loosened till all I could feel was my breath tickling the five o'clock shadow underneath my nose. For a seemingly endless moment, one summer evening, I was in complete control of my mind and the space-time continuum. A silky voice permeated my consciousness with instructions to "slowly open your eyes. Slowly."

The meditation was now over, and it was time to hear Kravag speak. During his "sermon," Kravag didn't refer to any notes or the Buddhist holy book. He spoke from the heart and told modern-day stories and analogies.

The basis of his lecture could be distilled to the basic concept that there is no real object outside consciousness unless perceived by another object. A chair is only a chair because we've given it that name. But what qualities make it a chair? What qualities exclude a tree stump from having the same qualities as a chair? People strive to make sense of certain circumstances surrounding death, birth, job loss, or various interpersonal relationships. They assign labels to each of these circumstances as "happy" or "sad" or "frustrating" because, in reality, that is how we're choosing to experience these events. But we have the choice to go through life cultivating a different kind of dialogue in our minds. Things usually labeled as "sad" or "tragic" can become opportunities to learn about oneself or help to ease the suffering of other people. We as a species can water the garden in our mind or let it become overrun with the suffocating weeds of negativity.

Kravag's words were timely, their meaning distilled perfectly to the current state of my life. I left that Buddhist teaching feeling for the first time in my life truly born again.

THE REV

The following week, I was due for a visit with my good high school friend Zach and his fiancée Joann. Late in the spring, they had mentioned that I would be participating in their July wedding as a groomsman. We were meeting to touch base on some last minute wedding details. However, when Zach picked me up at the train station he was Joann-less.

"Hey, dude," I said while wrapping my arms around my old friend, "where's your lady-friend?"

"She won't be joining us. I have something important to discuss with you," he said with a smile that bordered on mischievous.

"Oh, ho. Do tell, my friend. I'm intrigued," I expressed with delight as we got into his pickup truck.

"Nope," he said, waving me off with a solemn glare. "Not until lunch. Is Mexican okay?"

On the ride to the restaurant, I couldn't help but consider all the combinations and permutations of the mysterious and probable bad news he was going to dump on me.

(—*He's breaking up with her, dawg. It's either that or he's gay.*—)

(—He's not gay and he can't break up with her. She's great for him.—)

(—*Papi, he's gay, she knows, AND he's kicking you out of the wedding.*—)

(—He's totally got the hots for her. And why would he kick me out?—)

Halfway through our meal and all we'd managed was mindless chatter. While picking through the cornhusks of my tamales, hoping for more meat or masa he finally explained, "Joann and I, we don't want to you in the wedding party. You're not going to be a groomsman anymore." He spoke without any remorse. In fact, he looked rather pleased with himself dropping this bomb that threatened to completely destroy our friendship.

"What happened?" I asked with a lump in my throat that made me sound like a drunk Kermit the Frog impersonator. "What did I do…"

"Nothing," he said, his laughter making my discomfiture swell. "Dude, we want you to officiate the wedding. We want you to *do* the ceremony."

"What?" I asked, astonished at the instant change in my good fortune. "You can't be serious."

"Yes, I am. You're a good friend. And we thought you'd add some flair and theatricality to the ceremony," he said, placing his hand on my shoulder. "So, what do you say?"

"Yes. Yes! Of course, man. It would be an honor." I was delighted, like a little boy eating his way through a bag of Pixy Sticks while playing with his three new puppies at Disneyland on Christmas morning. I promised Zach all the flair and theatricality he could stand on the biggest and most important event of his life: poetry, candle lighting, a beautiful speech, and a team of monkey groomsmen. After Zach rejected my monkey groomsmen idea we agreed to collaborate on the ceremony together and I promised to find out how to get licensed as a minister (it had to be a legal wedding).

Upon arriving back at my apartment that evening, I searched online for organizations that offered ordination without requiring a class or church service, the thought of which was daunting after having attended some form of church activity nearly five thousand times in my youth. I found *The Universal Life Church*. Completing the arduous five-minute process of giving them my name, address, and credit card information, I became an ordained minister.

My title? Bishop Rivedal? Pastor or Priest? His Holiness or Eminence? Rabbi or Imam? Friar or Cardinal? These were all too extravagant. I am a man of the people. Reverend Rivedal or "The Rev" would do nicely.

I was now licensed in almost every U.S. state to perform weddings and funerals. In some cases I could even perform a Bris, and for my troubles... I could take tips (that joke never gets old). My decision to stay alive was looking sweeter and sweeter with each passing day.

THE CIRCLE OF LIFE

In the middle of my seventh grade year, at the Christian school that I attended, I got caught passing notes to some girls in my class. We were trying to make each other laugh by coming up with the dirtiest words we knew. Written on the paper were the words "masturbate," "pussy," "uterus," and "dick." I may have been the one who wrote "uterus" but I took the rap for everyone involved and immediately got sent down to the principal's office with the note.

The principal, Ms. Bilbo, an unpleasantly plump spinster who had been much friendlier as my second grade teacher, screamed at me to step into her office at once. "I cannot believe you, Joshua, you of all people," she said, spittle flying out of her mouth and onto the desk in front of her. "I expected more out of you. I had always thought of you as a leader, as someone who would grow up one day to become a famous minister, someone who would preach to thousands, maybe even millions. But there is no way you could ever amount to that, or anything else, writing notes like this," she said while shaking her fist at me. "I do not have much hope for your future anymore, Joshua. Now, get out of my office!"

* * *

The evening following my holy ordination, I called my mother to share the good news. "Well, you may be a minister in the eyes of the government, but you aren't in the eyes of God. You need a ministry," she said with a hint of contempt, satisfied with her perceived theological supremacy over her heathen, non-churchgoing son. Her assessment of my clerical legitimacy took the wind out of my sails. To be a true minister in her eyes, I needed to attend to the needs of others with tender love and kindness.

"But wait... I do have a ministry. Soon, I'm going to be speaking to hundreds, if not thousands of people this year about suicide prevention. I'm going to help people like you helped me." The thought that I would have become a true minister would've made Ms. Bilbo proud... or hungry.

"So you are," she said without the slightest hint of emotion in her voice. But I may have heard the corners of her lips crease upward. So be it and amen.

I'VE BEEN EVERYWHERE, MAN

Toward the end of that summer 2011, I put the finishing touches on a set of educational materials to accompany *The Gospel According to Josh:* Youth Suicide Prevention Program. During the fall semester of 2011, I was able to visit four universities and bring them my message.

All in all that first year I traveled to twenty different schools across the entire United States (including Hawaii). I made new and lifelong friends with whom I was able to commiserate, hold, and hug—a palatable array of sweet and savory tempered with a dash of bittersweet. I would never have savored the depth of any of these flavors if not for my father's suicide and my own near-death experience.

FALL 2012

In early September 2012, I began another year of school appearances with *The Gospel According to Josh* at Defiance College in Ohio. Setting up for the event, and while retrieving a few loose props at the bottom of my book-bag, my fingers grasped onto a crumpled piece of paper. It was brown and nearly falling to pieces from age. The scribble marks on the outside of the paper looked vaguely familiar. I unfurled the paper, delicately so, and discovered that the writing was mine. It was the sheet of paper that contained the three reasons why I had chosen to live, a page that took me on a quick trip eighteen months back into my dark past. I hadn't seen or thought about what was on this piece of paper in what had to be more than a year. Reading the writing of a desperate man, armed with only a glimmer of hope was utterly surreal.

1) I'll feel so guilty. If I kill myself, Erica and Jacob will probably be very upset. I can't let them lose their father and their brother... not like this.

2) There could be other adventures, many of them which I'll never experience... Macchu Picchu. Hawaii. Antarctica. Outer space.

3) *A family of my own. A soul mate... a happily ever after, a fairytale ending...*

Kneeling over my book-bag, I poured over those three little bullet points and was immediately filled with angst. I wondered if I'd ever achieve the last three words written on that paper. And then it hit me. So I jumped to my feet and crumpled that sheet of paper, and threw it high into the air into the blackness of the unlit stage behind me.

I had no need for fairytales, a puerile impracticality, forever out of reach. I was already living my own, and warts and all, it was shaping up to be a damn good one.

ABOUT THE AUTHOR

Joshua Rivedal is an actor, playwright, and international public speaker. He has spoken professionally about suicide prevention and mental health awareness in more than twenty-five U.S. states and two Canadian provinces. He wrote and developed the play, *The Gospel According to Josh*, which has toured extensively throughout the United States and Canada. He wrote the libretto to a Spanish language Christmas musical *Rescatando la Navidad*. As an actor, Josh has lent his voice to the role of Hippo in Scholastic's *Rabbit and Hippo In Three Short Tales*, the narrator of Julianne Moore's *Freckleface Strawberry and the Dodgeball Bully*, and numerous other audiobooks and animated projects.